ANARCHY OF CYBERTERRORISM:

**What you should know about
Cyber Crimes,
Cyber Espionage,
Cyber Attack,
Cyberwarfare &
Social Engineering**

ANARCHY OF CYBERTERRORISM:

What you should know about Cyber Crimes, Cyber Espionage, Cyber Attack, Cyberwarfare & Social Engineering

By

DR. TUNDE ALAOFIN

www.bookstandpublishing.com

Published by
Bookstand Publishing
Pasadena, CA 91101
4922_4

ISBN 978-1-956785-14-2

ACKNOWLEDGEMENTS

First and foremost, I want to give God all the glory for His mercy and unending love through Jesus Christ, my Lord and personal Savior, the creator of all knowledge and understanding. I would not be here today if it had not been for Him.

I'd like to convey my heartfelt gratitude and admiration to my parents, late Pa. Mathew Otitoju Alaofin and late Mrs. Florence Bamitale Alaofin, for their inspiration, direction, financial and emotional support, and many sacrifices that enabled me to reach this stage.

My heartfelt appreciation to my devoted, loving, and supporting wife. Your encouragements throughout the last two decades have been the driving force behind my success. It's been a tremendous source of comfort and relief to know that you were always there to assist with domestic duties while I worked. My deepest appreciation.

To my children, I am really appreciative of your patience throughout our busy schedules and trips. Thank you, gentlemen, for enabling me to spend time researching and writing away from you. You deserve another Disney vacation!

To all of my siblings, relatives, friends, and others who have helped me in one way or another, whether it was morally, financially, or physically, and who have shown their support in many ways. Thank you.

FOREWORD

In the past ten years, major cyberattacks have happened around the world. Almost like an equal-opportunity offender, these attacks have neither discriminated between the public or private sector, organizations, or private citizens, nor developed or developing countries. We all have been affected in one way or the other.

As an academic in the information systems and analytics area, I have always been fascinated with the adoption, diffusion, implementation, and use of modern information systems to achieve competitiveness in organizations. I have seen how properly leveraged digital strategies can create organizational renewal and attract undeniable returns on investment in these firms.

However, the current landscape of cyber-insecurity and cyberterrorism threatens the return on these massive technological investments in healthcare, education, government, corporate sector, and private citizenry. A McAfee report estimated global losses of cybercrime in 2020 to have topped $1 trillion! As it turns out, this is slightly over 1% of the world's GDP. Clearly, it is deeply concerning.

Anarchy of Cyberterrorism shines a light on this all-important pandemic. And did I say, "pandemic"? Yes, because cyber-insecurity is natively international in its reach and global in its scope. In his book, my colleague, Dr. Tunde Alaofin undertakes a careful explanation of the subject, object, and medium of cyberattacks. The book also proposes strategies for navigating the new crisis landscape.

The book is simple and straightforward. It does not delve into the complicated technical details but offers a clear understanding of the essentials of the subject matter. The author makes a careful intent to supply the reader with a well-supported and evidence-based text.

Leaders and managers of institutions will find this book really useful in understanding the basic underpinnings of Anarchy of Cyberterrorism. Nonetheless, it is really a book that just anyone should read.

Madison N. Ngafeeson, Ph.D.
Associate Professor of Information Systems & Business Analytics
Cisler College of Business, Northern Michigan University

TABLE OF CONTENTS

OVERVIEW

Cyberterrorism has been an issue of concern to individuals, government entities, and the world at large, especially during the COVID-19 pandemic. Cybersecurity involves the overall protection from criminal behaviors through technologies, systems, and processes aimed at protecting programs, systems, and networks from cyberattacks. Cyber-insecurity is characterized by increased cyberattacks and cyber threats following identified loopholes and vulnerabilities. The aftermath is compromised data and systems that could be detrimental to an organization's operations and national security. Cyberattacks refer to the attacks launched by cyber criminals through one or two computers while targeting a computer system or network and motivated by negative thoughts. Cyberattacks could also be motivated by financial or data theft, with disgruntled individuals capitalizing on the acquired money or data to disrupt computer systems. Cyberattacks could be undertaken by criminal groups and terrorist groups. Cyberattacks could also be undertaken by internal threats such as disgruntled employees, employees bypassing the required security policies, business partners, and competitors.

Dr. Tunde Alaofin

CYBER-INSECURITY AND CYBERTERRORISM

Cyber-insecurity poses a significant threat, especially in the modern world characterized by increased internet use. According to Morel (2021), Cybersecurity is a complex threat in the modern environment. The author highlighted the concept as the 100% phenomenon that human beings, without their knowledge, cannot fully resolve. Some people have encountered life-changing situations due to cyber-security concerns. Morel (2021) stated that some surveys denoted people as fearing Cybersecurity more than North Korea, climate change, and Iran's nuclear weapons. The increased vulnerability to cyber-insecurity in the modern era stems from the world's increased reliance on cyber states in operating crucial infrastructures and various life processes. Morel (2021) observed that Cybersecurity is associated with the technical complexities of internet technology and computer. Exploring the different cyberattack techniques and cyber-crime on governments and corporations requires the basic understanding of cyber-insecurity. Cyber-insecurity is a global problem affecting the various cyber systems and all the dependent infrastructures. According to National Research Council (U.S.) et al. (2010), cyber-insecurity emanates from the cyber systems' vulnerabilities, such as the flaws and shortcomings in the hardware and software as mitigated by the acts of the states, individuals, and groups using these systems. The text highlighted cyber-insecurity as taking the form of espionage, cyber warfare, attacks on cyber infrastructure, and cyber systems exploitation. The cyber-insecurity aspects have transnational components influencing the uses of cyber systems globally.

Cyber-insecurity impacts various life aspects, including government operations and corporation processes. Eze (2021) stated the effect of cyber-insecurity includes financial losses, litigation, damaged reputation, negative impact on share prices, deferred operational activities, and competitive disadvantages. Cybercrimes are often underreported, with organizations fearing the repercussions the report could have on the share process and the overall organizational performance. Eze (2021) noted that there are no definite means of determining the magnitude of the financial or data loss due to cybercrimes. Characteristically, the magnitude of a cyberattack depends on the attacked entity. Eze (2021) stated that the aftermath of cyberattacks on a local government would go beyond the financial impacts and data loss. The attack could result in the disruption of crucial city services and city infrastructures in various domains. The local or national government's inability to ensure Cybersecurity could sabotage the confidence of information society while increasing the government's vulnerability to various risks and threats. Challenges to reinforcing Cybersecurity differs for governments, organizations, and individuals depending on a country's context.

Cyberterrorism involves the politically instigated use of computers and information technology to instill fear and cause societal, national, or global disruption. Georgescu and Tudor (2015) noted that these political and deliberate attacks could be on communication networks, computer software, database, and computer systems. Cyber terror attacks and violence could harm individuals not associated with war. Georgescu and Tudor (2015) added that cyberterrorism could involve the terrorist organizations' reliance on information tactics and techniques that impact cyber-space. Cyberterrorists aim to impact the acts of real individuals in the real world with their virtual operations at cyberspace to influence these participants. Cyberterrorism's objective is to take over critical infrastructure networks associated with the air traffic, water supply networks, telecommunication, and financial systems. Terrorism and cyber warfare are some of the prominent threats in the modern world. The minimal understanding of cyberattacks and the growing terror threats increases the complexity of cyberterrorism as much as cyberterrorism is concerned. Georgescu and Tudor (2015) highlighted the importance of NATO and the European Union taking the right measures to uphold defense measures against terrorism and cyber warfare.

Socializing is an aspect of humanity and the social media age increasing loopholes in cyberterrorism. Riglietti (2017) outlined the ever-growing fear of cyberterrorism due to the increased online attacks. Cyberterrorism thrives on anonymity, with trackers able to bypass any aspects that make them easily traceable. The digital environment enables people to create and share knowledge that provides various avenues enabling people to commit cyber-crimes as offenders could be motivated to devise capabilities while exploiting vulnerabilities in the cyber environment. As the name denotes, cyberterrorism is a form of terrorism taking place in the cyber space, as undertaken through the internet and internet-based technologies and systems, with the targeted attack being critical infrastructures. Occasionally, Abeyratne (2011) noted that cyberterrorism uses computer networks to cause harm or attack critical infrastructures heavily relied on by the human population. The primary aspect of cyberterrorism is the intended harm and disruption of the ordinary societal operations. Riglietti (2017) highlighted cyberterrorism as denoting how the internet intensifies the capabilities of a terrorist organization through increasing its sustainability and ability to accomplish stipulated goals.

Cyberterrorism involves various cybercrime aspects, which could result in additional definitions that widen the concept. Marsili (2018) observed that going by some definitions, it could be difficult to differentiate the different online activities that could be termed as cyberterrorism and cybercrimes. Cyberterrorism could interact with ordinary terrorism, cybercrime, and cyber war. The article noted that when motivated by economic factors as opposed to ideological principles, it becomes cybercrime. The distinctive attributes of terrorism make it easy to differentiate cyberterrorism from cybercrime. Marsili (2018) highlighted the distinctive characteristics of terrorism as including instilling fear, using violence or the threat of violence, and the political motivation. However, an act that instills terror cannot be directly regarded as terrorism. The lack of a political motivation means that a cyberattack cannot be characterized as terrorism and ranks as a common crime. Cyberterrorism allows terrorist groups to advance their selfish agenda of disruption and causing harm to humanity using computer technology. Macdonald et al. (2019) stated that, unlike traditional terrorism, cyberterrorism strives to advance religious or ideological goals through physically or psychologically harming the children.

OVERVIEW OF DIFFERENT CYBERATTACK TECHNIQUES

Cyberattacks involve the efforts to steal, disable, and destroy information through unauthorized access to computers or network systems. The developing internet technology has increased the instances and diversity of cyberattacks. Kim et al. (2021) noted that cyberattacks are slightly deviating from traditional systems to cyber-physical systems (CPS). The article highlighted the increasing cyberattacks on smart homes and smart mobility. The article outlined the 2005 research findings on the critical vulnerabilities for self-driving cars. The researchers were able to remotely control and stop the self-driving cars while on the highway. Kim et al. (2021) highlighted the increasing sophistication and destructive aspects of the cyberattack techniques. Individual and state-sponsored are increasingly entering the cyberattacks field. Cyber attackers rely on hostile techniques in conducting complex attacks. Kim et al. (2021) highlighted the cyber attackers' utilization of offensive technology in complex attacks. Offensive cyberattacks are the hacking techniques targeting a system and not a defense technology. The article highlighted the importance of identifying cyberattack actors in gauging a cyberattack. Cyberattack actors include individual hackers, cybercriminals, hacktivists, cyberterrorists, and state-sponsored hackers.

Advanced infrastructures are increasingly prone to cyberattacks due to their heavy reliance on information technology. Mohammadi (2021) highlights smart grid as one of the infrastructures dependent on the advanced communication infrastructure due to the exchanged massive data amounts required to operate this complex system. As a result, smart grids are more vulnerable to cyberattacks. Communication systems drastically increase operation costs or damage the right operating systems. Mohammadi (2021) highlighted the case of Ukraine, where the 2015 attack on the country's power grids resulted in the widespread power outage for several hours. In ensuring the safe and proper operation of the smart grid, operators in power systems require to ensure efficient attacks detection and identification and upholding the right actions to the grid's protection. Ivanyo et al. (2018) stated that disruptions emanating from cyberattacks result in emergencies that could lead to loss of lives, environmental disasters, economic damage, and disruption of activities in cities. The increasing cyberattacks have necessitated the development of protection efforts. However, these efforts are not always effective in mitigating against cyberattacks. Ivanyo et al. (2018) noted that the shortcoming of most modern protection methods in tackling cyberattacks is that there is the use of signatures and prototypes from certain processes during the identification of attacks. Cyberattack forecasting fosters early protection and increased protection against cyberattacks.

The identified cyberattacks denoted the cyberattacks attributes. Kadivar (2014) highlighted actors as one of the attributes. The author noted that two actors are involved in a cyberattack. One of the actors is the owner of the targeted asset and the adversary. Targeted assets are the second attribute. These assets could include computer systems and networks. The third attribute is motivation. According to Kadivar (2014), the motivating factors in cyberattacks include acquiring the secure and unauthorized information and stealing data and money. The authors noted that the cyberattacks could be associated with security and political issues with the aim of sending propagandas. The fourth attribute is the impact on targeted assets. Kadivar (2014) noted that the effect on targeted assets could include the modification, deletion, or destruction of assets. The fourth attribute is duration. The article highlighted Owens, Dam, and Lin (2009) definition that denotes the possibility of a cyberattack continuing in an extended period.

The characteristics of the computer systems increase susceptibility to cyberattacks. Tellbach and Yan-Fu (2018) highlighted the vulnerability of two-way communication to cyberattacks that could not only affect the smart meters and the smart grids in their entirety. The authors classified cyberattacks into three various classes. These classes include availability, integrity, and confidentiality. The article outlined availability as a network enabling the normal communication performance. Tellbach and Yan-Fu (2018) highlighted that integrity is the second class referring to the network with protection from unauthorized change. The third class is confidentiality, which refers to the information being protected from unauthorized access. Wang et al., as cited by Tellbach and Yan-Fu (2018), outlined the additional classes of authenticity and non-repudiation. Authenticity refers to the network's ability to determine how genuine a message is. Non-repudiation denotes the user's inability to deny the message's reception.

Cyberattacks are challenging to resolve in its entirety. The unavailability of statistics on cyberattacks and individuals and organizations' failure to report these attacks have significantly hindered their resolution. Amir et al. (2018) highlighted that companies should report cyberattacks that could potentially damage business operations. However, organizations could underreport cyberattacks with managers underreporting these attacks and investors unable to independently discover these attacks. The article noted that reviews on data attacks between 2010 and 2015 denoted many disclosure attacks after investors know them. The revelation of data breaches in the market often occurs when customers whose information is stolen speak out. Amir et al. (2018) highlighted that the 300 cases of cyberattacks reported by public companies are relatively lower than those reported by independent entities. Data breach disclosure has a significant impact on organizational performance, a major concern for companies. Amir et al. (2018) observed that in instances where companies directly reported cyberattacks, there was a 0.33% decline in equity values three days after reporting and 0.72% in a month after the revelation.

Cyberattack Techniques

Cyberattack techniques refer to the malicious attacks aimed at unlawfully accessing data, disrupting operations, and destroy information. The cyberattack techniques could emanate from various actors, individual; and state-sponsored hackers, criminal, and terrorist groups. An understanding of cyber-threat techniques is instrumental in devising safeguarding measures for the individual networks, organizations, and governments. The below is a discussion of the common cyberattack techniques.

I.   Malware

Malware is an application intended to conduct various malicious tasks depending on the intention of the attacker. The malware injection could also go through several processes. The increased technology advancement and improved information access, with the aftermath being the increased cyber threats. Jang et al. (2020) defined malware as malicious software that harms computer systems and networks. A malware from one computer or network may end up spreading to other computers or networks. The assessment of a file containing a malware poses a significant threat to personal information held in the network and systems, necessitating the malware blockage before their execution. Jang et al. (2020) highlighted that every malware acts differently depending on the family origin, and the strategies to mitigate the malware are also different depending on malware family. Catak et al. (2021) stated that malware is deliberately formulated to destroy computer systems and networks and take advantage of weaknesses in the Cybersecurity system. Malwares have a predetermined target and strives to masquerade in an identity that could not be easily recognized, especially by individuals without adequate knowledge of computer networks, systems, and cybersecurity threats. Catak et al. (2021) observed that malware could take the form of file encryption, ransom, derailing the ordinary system operation, obtaining access to unauthorized networks, and data theft. The various platforms targeted by malware include servers, cameras, personal computers, networks, and mobile phones with the aim of derailing the systems' ordinary functionality. Catak et al. (2021) outlined malware development as an activity recently growing in sophistication, with 1046.10 million malwares reported in the early quarter of 2020. Malware could be avoided if only system developers put their selfish interests at bay and refrain from developing networks and computer systems and capitalizing on attractive features while bypassing potential weaknesses associated with the same.

Competition is the motivating factor with the manufactures and product development, and the desire to meet the increasing demand has resulted in the release of systems with security weaknesses that are increasingly prone to cyberattacks. Catak et al. (2021) stipulated that the malware's advanced competencies and diversity characteristics have necessitated the inclusion of cybersecurity efforts in organizations and government entities, with malware analysis being one of the cybersecurity activities. Being infected with malware does not mean that the organization has not capitalized on stringent Cybersecurity measures. Jasiul et al. (2014) stated that a Nomura Research Institute annual on Cybersecurity practices report highlighted that 100% of the organizations had anti-virus installations in their systems. Nevertheless, 30% of the organizations had cases of malware infections. The situation was not attributed to the unauthorized updating operating systems or having virus-infected files. Instead, it is due to the unavailability of signatures on the existing and available threats. Jasiul et al. (2014) observed that a significant proportion of malware contains known elements of malicious codes. Despite the difference in the installation packs for the malware, they have a similarity that could result in the launch of applications with different characteristics.

Malware injection into the computer system follows a lifecycle with a cybersecurity attack model. This model is divided into three steps. Walmor et al. (2021) highlighted malware injection stage as the first step in the process. During this process, the attacker infuses the malware into the targeted system by taking advantage of vulnerabilities such as removable media or weaknesses in the supply chain. The second step in the lifecycle is the command stage. Walmor et al. (2021) stated that the attack could make commands from a remote section while manipulating the malware in the targeted system depending on the intended reasons. During an attack on the AIS/ECDIS setup, the command is sent through modeled AIS messages. It is also during this stage that the malware keeps track of the information obtained through the radar or AIS with the aim of obtaining a pattern that is like the attack command. If the malware receives and recognizes the command, the next step takes place. The third step is the action stage. Walmor et al. (2021) stated that the malware exploits the radar or ECDIS calculation process during the action stage, depending on the transferred malware. The authors observed that some of the harmful acts undertaken during the action stage include a system rest, freezing the system, and record or replaying situations.

The malware trend and initiated processes in the targeted system are what increase their sophistication and impact in a network or computer system. Kim et al. (2021) highlighted the malware behaviors as including persistence, capturing videos, infusing network communications, and stealing information. The article compared the importance of malware in cyberattacks to bullets in war. Malware uses diverse technologies and cannot compare to other elements, with the complication denoted in the different steps of executing malicious codes. Obfuscation and packing are among the strategies for concealing malware, and recent use of the DLL Side-loading technique when hiding the technique and continuing to run the command. Kim et al. (2021) noted that the global perception of malware while consolidating with local characteristics could ensure accurate malware categorization.

The increasing sophistication of computer systems and advanced technology has been accompanied by increased instances of malware attacks. Catak et al. (2021) stated that there has been a significant increase in the number of malware activities from years 2011 to 2020. The article highlighted the use of different analysis techniques in formulating anti-analysis methods through the vast knowledge on anti-analysis strategies. The methods of evading analysis are often used to yield erroneous results. For anti-debugging methods often capitalize on developed pointer address parameters used in jump opcode. The use of anti-bugging techniques strives to derail malware samples from sunning under a debugger. The continued efforts to ensure early malware detection has resulted in automation. Catak et al. (2021) noted that the currently used automated malware detection systems are not always successful. The article highlighted the right malware labeling as one of the challenges characterizing the detection efforts. Using anti-virus applications for malware detection yields trojan, and a different anti-virus could be labeled as a worm. The complexities of malware detection have been the norm with the increased onset of sophisticated malware. Despite the malware changing its behavior and derailing the block dynamic analysis, some machine learning techniques could be used to determine malware families depending on the malware code. Catak et al. (2021) outlined the proposal by Ni, Qian & Zhang (2018) on the methods for malware categorization through using learning techniques. The proposal denoted an algorithm using the SimHash and CNN technique in malware classification. The algorithm alters the malware codes.

Detection techniques differ with age, with increased technology evolution resulting in the sophistication. However, Jang et al. (2020) highlighted the existence of two primary methods for malware detection. These methods are signature-based and heuristic-based, with the latter mitigating the disadvantages of the former. The authors observed that heuristic-based malware detection entails malware scanning to determine attributes suspected to be associated with malicious activities. Dynamic and static methods have also been developed in the malware detection efforts. Jang et al. (2020) noted that malware detection through the dynamic analysis method involves malicious behavior detection through the malware execution in a segregated virtual environment.

On the other hand, the static analysis method involves the malicious behavior detection through the identification of the entire structure without the malware's execution. Global image fosters detection of malware mutants through the maintenance of the overall structure while recognizes slight malware changes. Jang et al. (2020) outlined the similarity in the global images derived from malware in the same family, ensuring the suitability of malware classification. Therefore, the malware categorization narrows down on the frequency of malware discovery. Jasiul et al. (2014) observed that as per the Verizon Research, Investigations, Solutions, Knowledge (RISK) undertaken in 2012, in collaboration with different entities such as the Australian Federal Police denoted findings instrumental to resolving malware. The authors determined the 54% of malware were discovered after months, 29% after weeks, and 13% after days.

Malware could take different forms, with this document capitalizing on ransomware. With the ransomware program, files information is encrypted, and targeted victims are required to pay some considerable fees to acquire the decryption key. Sechel (2019) highlighted ransomware as a malicious application where infected files in a particular system are encrypted, and owners are required to make payments in cryptocurrency to receive the decryption key. Ransomware emerged from another program that would block victims from accessing infected systems and files while giving a message of the perpetrator masquerading as a state authority and demanding the victims to pay the ransom on the grounds of being found conducting illegal activities including video piracy. Sechel (2019) observed that from an operational angle, ransomware is a family of malicious applications used in the file and data encryption in various computer systems through complex symmetric and asymmetric algorithms. The modern ransomware executes several activities that differ depending on the ransomware family. The first activity is connecting the command with a control server (C2C) while necessitating the asymmetric RSA key pair development. Following the generation of the key pair, the ransomware downloads the public key C2C server. The second activity is the ransomware's generation of a symmetric key (SmKey) for the AES encryption algorithm. The third activity is the ransomware encrypting the data files in the affected system through the AES algorithm in the previous Symkey. Sechel (2019) stated that the fourth activity is the encryption of the AES Symkey with the previously downloaded.

The different ransomware families translated to the different encryptions. The article highlighted the different ransomware families as implementing various encryption forms depending on the actor's technical knowledge and capacity. Following the completion of the encryption process, the ransomware presents a message to the user on the steps to follow for the recovery of the encrypted files. In some ransomware, cryptocurrency payments could be required within a particular time. Sechel (2019) noted that derailing the countdown could be an unsuccessful strategy as the required PirivKey for decryption is not on the victim's system, and could be deleted, if the victim does not make payments within the required timelines. Arányi and Dávid (2021) highlighted that the growing cryptocurrencies and their increased exchange rate motivates its attractiveness as a ransom payment for cybercriminals. Various players in the internet industry are also legitimizing cryptocurrencies and including it as a payment form, increasing its preference as a payment mode in ransomware.

The growing ransomware has tagged along with the increasing acceptance in the use of cryptocurrency. Arányi and Dávid (2021) stated that the increased number of ransomwares has been characterized by the increased exchange rate of Bitcoin. The appreciation of the Bitcoin exchange rate influenced the frequency of ransomware attacks. The authors noted that in 2020, 1 Bitcoin was converted at USD 7185, with the same in April 2021 being at USD 62,926. The appreciated exchange rate intensified ransomware incidences. Incidences of ransom payments have been rampant globally. Arányi and Dávid (2021) observed that in 2019, victims paid EUR 10.1 billion in ransoms in the EU, which was 3.3 billion EUR more than in 2018. Ransomware detection is one of the difficult processes. However, Sechel (2019) highlighted the several detection and classification of malware. The first method is signature-based detection, where there is a comparison of the signature code against a database containing malicious signatures. Heuristic detection involves the comparison of suspect code functionalities against known malicious functionalities databases. Sechel (2019) observed that in machine learning, a supervised or unsupervised algorithm model is equipped to identify and classify new malware specimens depending on the similarity characteristics highlighted during training.

II. Phishing Attacks

Phishing is one of the cyberattack techniques resulting in financial losses for affected individuals, organizations, and governments. Like malware and other attack techniques, phishing is an increasing problem in the growing cyber industry. Jain et al. (2017) defined phishing as an attack where a perpetrator sends a fake email masqueraded as send from a reputable organization or entity. This email requires the recipient to fill out personal information such as phone numbers, passwords, emails, and usernames. The emails could pretend to be from reputable institutions such as banks and schools. Jain et al. (2017) observed that phishing messages are sent over messages, emails, and social media sites. However, emails are the popular phishing platforms, with 65% of phishing incidences emanating from the visits from the hyperlinks attached in the email. Rana (2020) defined phishing as social engineering technique utilizing several methodologies to influence the targeted victims to provide personal information that should not be shared, and which could compromise their personal information or finances. The attacker then uses the acquired information to the victim's disadvantage. Rana (2020) stated that the initial phishing incident was reported in 1995 with the attackers' use of phishing to convince their victims to provide their AOL account details. In 1997, the term phishing was first published on print media. However, phishing has subsequently grown over the years. Attackers are currently relying on recent media outlets. The article highlighted that by 2018, email-based phishing had declined to 1 in 3207 emails from 1 in 2995 in 2017.

Phishing techniques could also be in the form of web pages claiming to act on behalf of third parties. Eduardo et al. (2020) stated that the classification of phishing attacks is dependent on several considerations. One of the aspects is the attacked services, which could include banks, social networks, online payment platforms, online games, and cloud storage. The other consideration is the modus operandi. Such instances could include deceptive phishing, content introduction, and search engine phishing. In common phishing techniques of emails and webpages, the attackers used all manner of reasons to gain an advantage over their victims. Eduardo et al. (2020) observed that in phishing emails, victims are often told that they have won a reward and required to key in their personal information for the processing of the same. Through phishing websites, a victim receives a fake web page with minimal differences from the legitimate web page and a similar URL. Eduardo et al. (2020) highlighted the third technique as being the camouflaging links through the inclusion of special characters. In links using, symbols such as @ may be challenging to detect, especially for an actual observer. As a result, a user clicks the link believing it would lead to the ordinary Google page while it instead leads them to the browsers of the member page where they are required to input their personal information. From an attacker's perspective, the primary motives behind phishing attacks include financial gains, exploiting the stolen bank credentials for financial benefits, concealing the attackers' identity through the stolen information, and potentially selling the stolen identities to criminal who would prefer to conceal their identity in undertaking ordinary activities such as purchasing items online.

Determining users' behaviors increasing the surge in phishing attacks could foster measures to mitigate the menace. These measures could include training on to make users more informed on phishing attacks. Li et al. (2019) highlighted the non-homogeneity of education on users' security networks as increasing the susceptibility to phishing attacks in different magnitudes. Despite the claims by security and user experts that computers should not be reliant on users' behaviors, researchers determined the direct association between phishing and users' behaviors. As a result, one of the crucial prevention strategies is training on the adoption of security behaviors. Li et al. (2019) observed that user behavior education involves improving the internet user's phishing awareness and the defense mechanism. Education-based techniques provide online information or educational games. The simplicity of phishing attacks increases their success in their attacks as their victims do not have a lot to get around to and do not mind juggling. The authors outlined the 2011 discovery by Vishwanath et al. on the phishing emails having a peripheral processing while prompting an individual's decision making through the basic clues attached to the email messages. The findings denoted the urgency of the message ensures that the user bypasses other aspects that would help detect flaws.

The duration one has had with emails interaction determines their susceptibility to phishing attacks. Li et al. (2019) observed that users with more emails are more likely to be phished. However, the provided training is not primarily effective in curtailing phishing

18

attacks. Li et al. (2019) highlighted Vishwanath et al.'s proposition on modifying the security awareness and training angle. Instead, user education should capitalize on challenging and altering the misinformed thoughts and knowledge propelling the users' current behaviors, increasing their susceptibility to phishing attacks. The authors denoted the effectiveness of comprehending users' perspectives and decision--making techniques in implementing security awareness applications. Using interventions to comprehend user behaviors during phishing should capitalize on providing training on detecting fraudulent emails. The increased susceptibility is dependent on the used phishing technique and the prevailing strategy. Jain et al. (2017) highlighted the business-email compromise (BEC) as a significant threat in 2015. Through BEC, the attackers capitalize on spear-phishing techniques in targeting an individual or organization. When the user inputs their personal information in a fake webpage, the attacker uses this information for their selfish reasons. Jain et al. (2017) denoted the recent phishing detection efforts as resulting in new visual similarity-based techniques. The authors observed that this approach relies on various parameters in comparing the characteristics of a fake web page against a legitimate webpage.

The attackers do not directly launch their attack and make subsequent steps to ensure the success of their attack and acquire the required information. Ratsenis et al. (2020) highlighted the six primary steps in the email-based phishing attack. The first step is selecting the e-mail address. Before executing email-based phishing, an attacker needs to acquire the email of a potential victim. The attacker uses different e-mail selection strategies depending on the required number of e-mails and the targeted victims. The second phase is e-mail content creation. Ratsenis et al. (2020) outlined the preparation of e-mail content and text tailor-made to a particular victim. The second step is very important, with its categorization dependent on various criteria. The attacker needs to have an idea of the victim's involvement in the attack, have a strategy for generating the attacking e-mail, and determine the extent of the email personalization. The third step is sending the email to the selected target. Rastenis et al. (2020) highlighted the methods of sending the email as an essential factor. The implementation of the chosen phishing attack strategy is through sending the phishing e-mails. The e-mail sending step has three basics criteria: the number of targeted victims in the phishing attack, a systematic phishing attack strategy, and the sender's e-mail address. The article denoted the e-mail address selection strategies as classified into two main categories: using available e-mail addresses or generating e-mail addresses.

III. SQL Injection

SQL injection is another common cyberattack technique. This technique disrupts the inquiries that a user, through the database, makes to an application. Clarke (2012) observed that SQL injection is an attack involving the insertion of a SQL code into an application or any other input parameter at a user's disposal. The code is later sent to a back-end SQL- server to follow additional execution instructions. Any process that develops SQL statements is susceptible as the diversity of SQL and the various methods available for its construction yield several coding options. Clarke (2012) stated that the initial form of SQL injection requires directly inserting the code into parameters that have SQL commands. Sarkar (JJJ) outlined SQL injection as one of the many mechanisms that hackers use when stealing data from organizations. The technique is among the common layer application attacks currently in use. Sarkar (2018) noted that SQL injection capitalizes on improper coding in a web application, enabling a hacker to inject SQL commands into a login form enabling access to data maintained in a database. The prominence of the SQL injection is due to available fields for user input allows the passage of SQL statements to place a direct query in the database.

The SQL injections follow the legitimate path used by credible application users as they seek database access. Sarkar (2018) highlighted web applications as allowing access to legitimate visitors to submit and obtain data to or from a database through the internet while using the preferred browser. Databases are central points in modern websites as they are storage sites for data needed by websites for the delivery of content to visitors and providing information to customers. Some of the resident information in the database includes user information, financial statements, and company statistics. Legitimate users access the resident information in the database through off-the-shelf or custom web applications. As a hacking technique, SQL injection strives to pass SQL commands through the backend database. Sarkar (2018) stated that in the absence of a proper sanitization method, web applications could result in SQL injections allowing hackers to access information from the database and modifying some. The website features of login pages, support and request forms, and shopping carts are vulnerable to SQL injections due to the available user input, a passage of SQL statements.

The changing aspects of internet use are increasingly introducing more Cybersecurity challenges due to created vulnerabilities and loopholes. Zhao and Liu (2020) observed that following the introduction of web2.0, the internet ensures convenience while increasing harm. The authors detailed OWASP's 2017 publication on "Top Ten Security Vulnerabilities List" as listing SQL injection attacks as remaining the most harmful vulnerabilities. Currently, many websites are heavily reliant on WAF defense technology while ignoring the need to elevate the code quality. Zhao and Liu (2020) associated the trend with most security developers lacking security awareness and do not standardize the writing of SQL statements and filter special characters during the program development process. The aftermath is the client's ability to render SQL statements using GET and POST variables to initiate normal execution. Despite SQL injections being common, they should not be ignored due to their impact at the organizational or individual level. Chen et al. (2021) highlighted the SQL injection attack on Sony's PlayStation Network in

April 2011. The attack affected more than 77 million accounts, and 12 million credit cards were stolen. During the attack, the stolen information included passwords, user accounts, and addresses. Records on credit card spending were also leaked to the public, with the aftermath being Sony's indirect loss of 170 million USD. "Rasputin," a Russian hacker, relied on SQL injection vulnerabilities to access the database server and take over the system during the February 2017 attack. Chen et al. (2021) observed that SQL injection attacks also resulted in a substantial lot of sensitive information stolen in close to 20 universities and agencies in the UK and the US. A web application that is database-driven faces a substantial threat of SQL injection. The SQL injection attack is like a user's ordinary system access and could be enabled by submitting Web forms or page requests.

SQL injection detection is crucial for web-applications, considering most of them are associated with critical infrastructures. As a result, their attack could cripple important operations and compromise national security. Term Frequency Inverse Document Frequency (TFIDF) algorithm is one of the options for SQL injection detection. Li and Zhang (2019) noted that the TFIDF algorithm is a weighted technology to data-mine and retrieve information. This algorithm examines the essence of a word document in a file set. The document becomes essential depending on the number of appearances in the file set. However, the decrease is also dependent on the appearance frequency. Li and Zhang (2019) observed that in the use of TFIDF algorithm, it takes the term frequency and inverse document frequency. In vectorizing the text in SQL statements, the algorithm utilizes a particular basis. The frequency appearance in attack statements and rare occurrence in normal statements denotes the word's good ability in recognition of abnormal classes. As a result, the algorithm is used in undertaking SQL statements vectorization depending on the sensitivity of characters and keywords. The complexity of the SQL attack statements has been necessitated by the nature of the attack statements. Aruna and Usharani (2020) observed that SQL systems are highly flexible, and attackers could easily change the attack's presentation and evade the detection systems. The hacker could inject the malicious SQL command in the web application's original query, initiating their execution in the server. The entry into the system allows the hacker to run malicious codes in the system and executing most of these codes and launching attacks against the database and server.

CYBERTERRORISM AND CYBERCRIME ON GOVERNMENTS

C ritical infrastructures run by most governments are interconnected by networks and computer systems, making them prone to cyberterrorism. The aftermath of these attacks has a ripple effect on the general population, with incidences of violence, damaged properties, and deaths. The societies increasing dependence on technological systems has created vulnerabilities that are easily used by terrorist groups. Weimann (2004) traced cyberterrorism back to the 1990s, during the rapid growth of internet technology. The article noted that despite cyberterrorism not being directly associated with violence; its psychological impacts on societies have effects equating to terrorist bombs. Luca (2017) highlighted the evolving nature of cyberterrorism and its impact on a government. According to the federal bureau investigation (FBI), the article highlighted that cyberterrorism is a predetermined attack propelled by political reasons and targeting information, computer systems, software, and data, resulting in attacks against noncombatant groups. Luca (2017) noted that cyberterrorism is a consolidation of terrorism and cyberspace, taking the forms of threats against computers, networks, and stored information. Cyberterrorism aims at intimidating or coercing a particular country's government or population to advance social or political agendas. Cyberterrorism is one of the recent forms of political and social sabotage, with the governments being the primary targets. Klein (2015) highlighted Barrack Obama's acknowledgment of threat from cyberterrorism as a cybersecurity challenge posing a significant threat. The unfortunate thing is the lack of a clear definition of cyberterrorism. To qualify as cyberterrorism; an attack could result in violence targeting individuals, property, or cause. Klein (2015) observed that when considering the severity of effects, computer attacks with a limited scope could result in deaths, injury, water contamination, air crashes, or the general population losing faith in the economy qualify as cyberterrorism.

Cyberterrorism does not include hacking activities such as hacktivism. Klein (2015) defined hacktivism as a term entailing the combination of hacking and political activism. Like in hacking, hacktivism involves activities undertaken online to manipulate and reveal vulnerabilities in computer networks and systems. Hacktivism, despite being propelled by political reasons, does not qualify as cyberterrorism. Discussions on cybercrimes involving the government could be discussed from two perspectives. The first is a government being the perpetrator of cybercrime targeting other governments and to obtain a trade or relational advantage. The second perspective is the government being the target of cybercrime attacks. Hill and Marion (2016) attributed the increase in cybercrimes to advanced computer technology and the internet. The Internet has become an essential component of operation for individuals, corporations, institutions, and the government. Governments can efficiently and effectively conduct its operations while manning its critical infrastructures. The advanced technology has created opportunities for cybercrimes, with enemy countries using new and traditional criminal tactics over the cyberspace. Hill and Marion (2016) observed that cybercriminals can easily hack their way into any computer system worldwide at minimal cost and a slight chance of detection. The surging incidences of cybercrimes targeting opponent governments crate the possibility of cyberwar with allied countries joining forces against their opponents.

Individual countries have made considerable investments in cybercrime prowess as an advantage over other governments. Ortner (2015) highlighted Russia as boasting a professional and lucrative cybercrime industry, with Russian hackers taking responsibility for a significant proportion of cybercrimes. The author highlighted the Russian government's refusal to sign the Council of Europe Convention on Cyber Crime due to the reluctance to investigate the many cyberattacks caused by the Russian citizens and using the government's infrastructure. Russia could be blamed for its contribution to the transboundary through its direct involvement or its complicity in cybercrime. Ortner (2015) stated that Russia was accused of being directly responsible for Estonia's 2007 and 2008 cyberattacks. The tools that hackers used during the attack were stored in government servers, while the infrastructures and servers used in the attack had government IP addresses. The Russian government in perpetrating cybercrime could also be denoted in the preventive measures the country employs. Ortner (2015) noted that the Russian government utilizes a considerable cash flow to install anti-virus and anti-phishing tools while excluding efforts to arrest perpetrators and derail the actual attacks. The country has legislation criminalizing cybercrimes. However, the penalties could be too low to deter cybercrimes.

Government websites host several critical infrastructures and information detrimental to national security. Governments could be reluctant to acknowledge cyber-crime attacks and blame them on their citizens. Kshetri (2013) highlighted the Chinese government as commonly blaming foreign countries for cyberattacks targeting the country. The article gave the example of the claims by Gu Jian, the Chinese Ministry of Public Security, who claimed to experience cyberattacks on 200 Chinese governments daily, and which were foreign based. The Information Office of the State Council stated that more than one million IP addresses were controlled, and 42,000 websites being subjects of cyber-crime attacks from foreign-based hackers. The article highlighted the Chinas Computer Emergency Response Team (CNCERT) report that detailed the country's 8.9 million as attacked by 47,000 foreign IP addresses. Ray and Kaushik (2017) highlighted Hacktivism as the most prominent form of cyberspace attacks targeting the government, making up 60% of attacks targeting government assets. Kshetri (2013) highlighted the alleged reports of the Chinese government agencies participating in cyberattacks with their targets being domestic businesses and consumers. The authors highlighted examples of claims about Chinese government agencies using viruses to attack banned websites. Kshetri (2013) outlined the alleged claims of Myanmar and Mauritania governments hiring botnet operators to attack the websites of their critics with DoS attacks. The Myanmar government was claimed to have built a fully-fledged and advanced cyber warfare department as part of the police operations.

Alleged claims of various governments' involvement in cyber-crime attacks and developing weapons to serve the same purpose elicit the question of the role played by governments in the cyber war. Denning (2012) highlighted the claims of the United States and Israel's development and deployment of Stuxnet. Several news-press headlines had termed Stuxnet as the game changer. The article observed that compared to other computer worms, Stuxnet non-selectively spreads from one vulnerable computer system to another. This computer worm is differentiated from others in that it is formulated to release its payload on entering an industrial control system (ICS) with similar characteristics to Iran's nuclear enrichment entity. On entering the facility, the article noted that the worm destroys the programmable logic controller (PLC) code in charge of the centrifuges at Natanz. The aftermath is the destruction of close to a thousand centrifuges and a disruption of the nuclear program in Iran. The systems created to secretly conduct government attacks could get into the hands of civilians, resulting in substantial impacts. Denning (2012) highlighted that before Stuxnet, Vitek Boden, which targeted the Maroochy Shire Council sewerage system was a complex cyberattack with significant effects on an ICS. The 2000 Queensland attack in Australia was propagated by one of the employees from the company contracted to develop the system. The employee used the software and equipment from the company to access the ICS network and modify data. Denning (2012) noted that the attack on the government's sewerage system resulted in pumps' malfunction and the pump turning off. This failure resulted in raw sewage, the death of marine life, and the harmful effects on the environment.

The attacks on government systems are sophisticated and could significantly affect the operations and the population at large. Governments, individuals, and corporations are overly reliant on communication information systems (CIS). Cybercriminals target a system that they know would totally cripple the system and send the ripple effect. Limba et al. (2017) noted that cyber criminals focus on critical infrastructure since a successful attack could result in them benefitting financially and politically. The advancing sophistication of cyberattacks is due to the overreliance on CIS and technologies. Cyberattacks on infrastructures could affect both the government and private sectors reliant on government systems for operations. The authors highlighted the case of the December 2015 attack targeting the Ukrainian power supply system, cutting off 225,000 users. The US Department of Homeland Security highlighted that the execution of the attack was through malicious software. Limba et al. (2017) observed that the attack was the first successful cyberattack that resulted in a power interruption. The article highlighted the unsuccessful efforts to determine the source of the attack due to the challenge of people claiming responsibility for cyberattacks.

Most countries do not have a comprehensive strategy to respond to cyberattacks that make them unprepared to resolve unforeseen scenarios and vulnerabilities. Limba et al. (2017) stated that government organizations such as the U.S Department of Energy and the U.S Department of Homeland Security focus their attention on the primary attacks on critical infrastructures or industrial control systems (ICS). The authors' classified attacks into five major categories depending on the objectives achieved on the targeted system. These five classifications are also the motivating factors for the attacks targeting government systems. These include.

a) Information corruption. This change occurs following an improper alteration of data in a system or communication channel.

b) Denial of service (DoS). Denying authorized users access to data or communication systems.

c) Information disclosure. Such attacks involve the disclosure of information to unauthorized individuals such as the general population or a neighboring county. Such acts could be detrimental to national security and government operations.

d) Theft of resources. Attacks resulting in the system resources being used by unauthorized parties.

e) Physical destruction. When the use of ICS results in the destruction of properties and physical harm.

Limba et al. (2017) highlighted the US Department of Energy and Department of Homeland Security's prediction on the changing cyber environment, resulting in the change to the attack vectors targeting critical infrastructures, necessitating the government to combat emerging threats. The government operations are more prone to cyberattacks due to the involved populations, and the national security policies need to prioritize the protection of these infrastructures. Jensen (2010) noted that 98% of all U.S government communications operate over networks that are operated and owned by civilians. The U.S government is not in charge of these networks. The article noted that network systems running government operations lack adequate security and protection, in addition to the civilian computer systems, which led to Admiral McConnell's prediction of the United States suffering from the "electronic Pearl Harbor." McConnell further added that the United States would need to go through reinvention to include and bear the accountability for the advancing technology.

The cyberattacks target both developed and developing countries. Attacks do not solely focus on the United States and the United Kingdom. Jensen (2010) noted that countries like Zimbabwe, Iran, Israel, Tatarstan, and South Korea have been victims of cyberattacks. Additional famous cases include the Estoma in 2007 and Georgia in 2008. In both incidences, the cyberattacks totally crippled the government's ability to run its operations. The Estonia attacks narrowed down to the government websites, civilian infrastructures, and the banks in the country. Jensen (2010) outlined the coordinated attacks on the Georgian government, media, and banking sector before the invasion by the Russian troops. The authors noted that the detailed attacks denoted the possibility of government attacks and natural consolidation of cyberattacks with kinetic attacks. The U.S communications undertaken through civilian-operated and owned systems has both classified and unclassified information, a potential target by cyber criminals. Jensen (2010) noted that the communication in these networks could include military objectives and instructions on undertaking military operations. The author pointed out that the communication could also include current intelligence and information reports from the battlefield to inform strategic decision-makers in the Pentagon, among other headquarters. In ordinary armed conflicts, military objectives in communication are a probable target. Jensen (2010) observed that the military objectives as defined by Article 52 of the API.63 Article 52 with the title *General protection of civilian objects* illuminate those civilian objects should not be points of target. Communication and technology systems belonging to the military or intelligence agency, including computers, networks, and routers, are used in fostering military communication. The article noted that if these communication objects were undertaking the same functions for the civilians and not the government, the received protection would equate to that of the civilian objects. However, their use in military or intelligence agency activities makes them a target.

Critical infrastructures are often under the government's operation and management, with their massive population coverage making them a potential target for cyberattacks. The critical infrastructures that make human life possible are very vulnerable to cyberattacks. Miron and Muita (2014) defined critical infrastructures as systems and assets that are crucial to the citizens' safety and wellbeing. These assets include water, fuel and electricity production and distribution systems and communication channels. Disruption of one of the highlighted critical infrastructures results in financial costs and potential loss of lives, which is the reason for the attacks and the reason the cyberattacks criminals target these assets for political and profit reasons. Most cyberattack threats towards the government equate to attacks targeting critical infrastructures. Miron and Muita (2014) observed that with the increasing sophistication and interdependencies in critical infrastructures, providers need to grapple with increasing vulnerabilities to mitigate cyber threats. Three aspects could include the vulnerabilities to these infrastructures. The first is the direct infrastructure effect. The authors observed that this effect could be in the form of the flowing disruption or withholding functions of the infrastructure by attacking critical systems or functions. The second is the indirect infrastructure effect. Miron and Muita (2014) noted that this effect includes the trickling effect due to how the government, society, and the economy react to the cyber-crime attack. The third effect is infrastructure exploitation. This effect involves utilizing a particular infrastructure as the gateway to disrupting or destroying another related target.

The current and emerging threats necessitate the continuous implementation of Cybersecurity by the government, industry stakeholders, and crucial infrastructure providers. The impact of cyberattacks targeting government infrastructures is also dependent on targeted assets. HHH observed the unpublicized cyberattacks targeting infrastructure services, with the attribution of these processes requiring sophisticated and uncertain processes necessitating well-developed skills and capabilities to determine the actors of the said crimes. However, the publicized attacks show that there are many actors behind cyberattacks targeting water systems. These actors could include hacktivists performing cyberattacks as motivated by their political ideologies, dissatisfied former employees, revenge missions, cybercriminals motivated by financial gains, and hackers conducting attacks for fun. Amoros (2013) noted that national infrastructures, especially those in the United States, have always been vulnerable to malicious physical attacks, including theft, vandalism, equipment tampering, asset theft, and facility bombing. The 11th of September 2001 events are the most outstanding physical attacks directed towards national infrastructure. In recent years, most of the national infrastructure have become reliant on information technology, including software, computers, and networks. The reliance included remote access through the internet to control national services. Amoros (2013) observed that rivals can now easily attack infrastructure by deploying worms and viruses. These attacks could target the national infrastructures by being initiated from automated control systems.

Government protective measures could exploit the advanced technology system through detection systems, antivirus software, and encryption. Clark and Hakim (2017) highlighted the increasing concern of policymakers on cyber threats to the United States infrastructure, among other assets. Information communication technology (ICT) is becoming an ordinary phenomenon in the US, with the increasing interdependence among ICT devices and other components. As a result, an interference in one component could lead to a negative ripple effect on others. Clark and Hakim (2017) noted that damaged critical infrastructure due to cyberattacks could significantly impact national security, the economy, and the general population's wellbeing. Additional actors targeting the government infrastructures in cyberattacks could include cyber-spies pilfering classified information critical to the government operations as a means of obtaining a competitive, security, or financial advantage. Cyber-warriors could be acting as agents of their countries to undertake cyberattacks that would favor their country's strategic objectives.

CYBERTERRORISM AND CYBERCRIME ON CORPORATIONS

C yberattacks as undertaken by terrorist groups significantly impact business operations and the overall performance of corporations. Information communication technology (ICT) is increasingly becoming a tool for ensuring efficiency and effectiveness in undertaken tasks while ensuring a competitive advantage in the industry. Cyberterrorism is affecting the operations of corporations as it does in government through exploiting available vulnerabilities. In the past, businesses and organizations feared thieves who could potentially push them out of business by any goods at their disposal. However, businesses and corporations fear digital theft in the modern day with the rise in cyber-crimes and cyberattacks. Cyberterrorism is threatening business and corporation operations. Organizational leadership have not only to worry about market growth and increasing revenues but also the increasing threat of cyberterrorism. Afshani (2019) noted that cyberterrorism is one of the threatening forms of terrorism. Companies are no longer worried about the physical theft of data and properties. The author noted that in the internet age, companies are more concerned about their software being compromised by online hackers. Afshani (2019) observed that in the recent decade, hackers have succeeded in intruding security systems of even global companies such as Yahoo, Amazon, and Microsoft. Most organizational processes are conducted online, increasing vulnerability to cyberterrorism and cyberattacks. As a result, organizations are investing in a complex security system to safeguard against data compromises. Afshani (2019) observed that companies have a higher risk of disrupted online services and the theft of confidential information even with high-level security systems. Companies often avoid reporting cyberterrorism and cyberattack incidents due to the fear these repercussions could have on the organizational performance and the public goodwill.

Reports of cyberterrorism and cyberattacks significantly impact stock prices in these companies. Afshani (2019) observed that according to research, companies experience an average 2% loss due to cyberattacks. An individual with minimal understanding of cyberterrorism and cyberattacks may question why companies are putting themselves at the line of these attacks. ICT is an essential aspect of modern business operations. Olănescu and Olănescu (2019) highlighted that in the current social and economic settings, private companies are increasingly interconnected through IT structures. The importance of IT in business operations means the lack of the same could be a disadvantage to a given organization. Gao and Zhong (2015) outlined the current advancement of information and communication technologies. The absence of these technologies could eliminate the presence of commerce and entertainment industries. Businesses of many organizations are overly dependent on information systems in an electronically networked world. Firms in the tourism and hospitality industry are among those heavily dependent on IT. Arcuri et al. (JJJ) highlighted tourism and hospitality as significantly impacted by the growing information and communication technologies. Through the growth in ICT, it is easy to connect tourists with hospitality businesses. The authors highlighted the emergence and inclusion of ICT in the hospitality industry as crucial for business operation and fostering the achievement of the sustainable development goals (SDGs) as approved by the United Nations. Arcuri et al. (JJJ) stated that some of the SDGs that could be achieved include SDG 9 on industry, innovation, and infrastructure and SDG 17 on fostering global partnership for sustainable development.

Organizations rely on different information systems, which could explain the difference in the magnitude of cyberterrorism and cyberattacks. Gao et al. (2014) highlighted the complex and dynamic nature of information systems relying on modern computer systems and networks. The authors noted that this complexity provides numerous opportunities for data misuse by cyber-criminals. The sophisticated reliance on information technology necessitates companies' investment in cybersecurity infrastructure to safeguard their client information and safeguarding its interests. Haapamäki and Sihvonen (2019) highlighted the consideration of the role of cybersecurity as a risk management aspect to mitigate the increasing cyber threats and risks. In examining cyberterrorism in an organization, it is essential to have a better understanding of the concept. Olănescu and Olănescu (2019) stated that an online space activity could be classified as cyberterrorism if it has an aspect of terror and political motivation. As cited earlier in the text, cyberterrorism is different from cybercrime in that the former is a preconceived and politically motivated act targeting information and computers systems. Just like in ordinary attacks, organizations need to examine cyberterrorism and cyber-crime attacks to determine the extent of the damage and determine the right course of action.

Examining the nature of the damage is part of the larger cybersecurity strategy that needs consideration by organizations. This strategy is implemented as a safeguarding strategy and not primarily to resolve attacks that have already occurred. However, this strategy can come in handy in dealing with the already occurred attacks. Cybersecurity has emerged as one of the risk challenges encountered by organizations in modern society, and which require adequate management. Haapamäki and Sihvonen (2019) acknowledged the severity of cybersecurity as an organizational concern that could be resolved through its integration as part of a managerial control system. As part of this control system, cybersecurity is a crucial managerial accounting and auditing issue requiring an internal control assessment and the cost-benefit analysis. Haapamäki and Sihvonen (2019), as cited by Gordon and Loeb (2006), classified cybersecurity objectives into three primary categories. The first is cybersecurity as a protection of confidential information and the second as a means of ensuring that only the authorized individuals access the information. In the third category, cybersecurity ensures that the information in an organization is accurate, reliable, and valid. The extreme costs of cyberattacks necessitate cybersecurity risk management in organizations. Cybersecurity as part of organizational management could be necessitated by government regulations. Haapamäki and Sihvonen (2019) highlighted the Sarbanes-Oxley Act of 2002 (SOX) as imposing strict performance on organizations. The SOX regulation denotes the importance of information system controls through the requirement of the leadership reporting on the effectiveness of internal controls. Sales (2013) equated cybersecurity to environmental law, and the former should embrace the seriousness characterizing the implementation of the latter. The similarity stems from the two sectors being impacted by negative externalities. The reluctance in the implementation of environmental conservation efforts is replicated in cybersecurity. Sales (2013) noted that the underinvestment in pollution controls are replicated in the underinvestment in cyber-defenses. The firms' inability to fully cater to the costs of their vulnerabilities results in weaker incentives in securing the systems.

Currently, organizations operating through the internet and using computer systems and networks cannot assume that they are safe from cyberterrorism and cyberattacks. Stevenson (2004) highlighted the importance of determining the extent of an attack after its occurrence. The absence of concrete valuation techniques makes it difficult to collect adequate information on the attack and take the required measures in tackling the issue and curtailing the activities after the attack from resulting in additional losses. Stevenson (2004) stated that unauthorized losses from cyberattacks could emanate from the unauthorized destruction or sale of information and the destruction emanating from malicious software introduced to a network or computer system. Losses from cyberterrorism or cyberattack could be tangible or intangible. Stevenson (2004) that losses are considered tangible if they can be associated with direct costs of material or labor changes. However, the author noted that the significant damage from a cyberattack emanates from the losses associated with the intangible aspects of an attack. One of the post-attack activities firms could opt to disclose the damage depending on the potential impact on the organizational operations. Amir et al. (2018) stated that firms should open on the material damage of cyberattacks on business operations. However, the author noted that since investors cannot independently learn about cyberattacks, organizational leadership tends to conceal the information on cyberattacks from the investors or even underreport the same. The article noted that following a review of information on cyberattacks conducted between 2010 and 2015, the findings displayed that most attacks were disclosed after investors discovered them. The different reactions to disclosed information determine the manager's handling of information on cyberattacks. Amir et al. (2018) noted that managers reveal the occurrence of an attack when investors have a 40% certainty of occurrence and conceal information due to the higher uncertainty on a cyberattack.

Cyber-risk attacks and disclosure of the same is dependent on the industry of a particular firm. Pooser et al. (2018) observed that increased cyberattacks have resulted in regulatory bodies increasing their oversight on firms discharged with the function of storing sensitive information. The article highlighted the National Association of Insurance Commissioners (NAIC) proposal on an *Insurance Data Security Model Law* to be followed by state regulators through the development of threshold on data security investigation and confirmation of a data breach occurrence. The difference in the cybersecurity measures is denoted in the banking industry. Pooser et al. (2018) outlined the March 2005 order from the federal banking regulators as the regulatory standards characterizing the U.S banking sector. The increasing risk posed by the continued cyberattacks and cyberterrorism has necessitated corporations considering cyber risk insurance policies. The authors highlighted the general concern by managers and CEOs on the potential liability posed by cyberattacks. The banking corporations are increasingly concerned by the adverse effects of cyberattacks due to this industry's vulnerabilities to these attacks.

Financial institutions are more potential targets of cyberattacks compared to other corporations. Skinner (2019) stated that cyberattacks are challenging risks characterizing financial institutions in the modern age. These attacks present cyber risks that result in corporate governance challenges requiring management and threats on financial stability requiring mitigation by the financial regulators. The author noted that the banking sector provides services including payments, credit, and demand deposits. The highlighted services are instrumental to the performance of the general economy. As a result, the bank's vulnerability to cyberattacks poses a threat to distortion of critical services resulting in ripple effects that could impact the performance of the general economy. Skinner (2019) highlighted the sentiments of Kevin Stiroh, the New York Fed's Executive Vice President of the Financial Institution Supervision Group. According to Kevin, nobody needs to be convinced of cyberattacks being a fundamental financial risk for financial entities, financial systems, and the entire economy. Instead, cyber risks are a perfect case of a situation requiring interventions through financial regulation and ensuring a stringent cybersecurity system. Skinner (2019) noted that the bone of contention is on designing the financial regulation intervention. The Securities and Exchange Commission (SEC) is one of the financial regulators that have increasingly focused on cyber risks.

The banking laws and regulations have remained unchanged in the face of the increasing cyber risk due to the many cyberattacks and cyberterrorism incidents. However, SEC has made significant progress. Skinner (2019) noted that in February 2018, the commission strengthened a regulatory guidance initially issued in 2011. In the guidance, Jay Clayton, the SEC chairman, clarified the need for public companies focusing on cybersecurity issues and taking the proper measures, and ensure communication to investors on material cyber risks and incidents in a timely manner. The 2018 SEC guidance articulated the companies bearing obligations as per the Securities Act of 1933 and Securities Exchange Act of 1934 on revealing cyber controls, risks, and vulnerabilities. Many entities were unsure of the legitimacy of the reasons SEC put forward on the public companies under disclosure of cyber risk. Many companies are reluctant in disclosing cyber breaches incidents.

Several companies have experienced significant data breaches due to cyberattack incidences and portrayed reluctance in communicating the issue to investors and other stakeholders until the victims of the attacks publicized the incident. The cyberattacks of recent years have resulted in financial losses and massive leakages of sensitive data. Tariq (2018) highlighted that according to Group-IB expert evaluations, at least 99% of all the cyber-crimes in the world today involve money theft. The author noted that 2017 was an outstanding year for identity thieves, as the massive malware attack in the year destroyed many companies, including DLA Piper, Rosneft, EVRAZ, Russian banks, and Maersk in India, including many other victims in different countries. Tariq (2018) stated that Equifax is one of the countries that experienced massive data breaches in 2017. During the attack, all the wrongly acquired sensitive information could potentially be used for identity theft. The company was distinctive in its manner of managing the incident. Skinner (2019) observed that Equifax delayed for months without informing its customers that the company had encountered a significant cyberattack that impacted at least 143 million Americans. Cyberattacks have disastrous impacts on individuals and business operations and require more attention than it received in the past. Organized and specialized groups have been

41

robbing money and data from financial institutions through the assistance of malware. These groups could be more motivated on the silence of these institutions with regards to cyberattacks, increasing their vulnerability. A timely disclosure following cyberattack incidents should be a requirement pressed on financial and non-financial, private, and public companies through regulatory interventions.

Cyberattack is a widespread menace in the financial institutions. The case was worse when the incident hindered the acquisition of services. Tariq (2018) highlighted the reporting of the cyberattack by the New York Times and people's reactions on the same. The article outlined the surging frustrations with the customers from Bank of America, JP Morgan Chase, Citigroup, and Wells Fargo were unable to access their accounts or conduct online bills payments. The frustrations also stemmed from the fact that the banks had failed to explain what was happening. During the attack, the actors' objective was to conduct theft that would lead to any financial loss. Instead, the attack aimed at frustrating the customers and resulted in a financial disadvantage. The article cited the CNN description of the Denial of Service as an effective yet unsophisticated attack technique that does not involve any form of hacking. During the highlighted cyberattacks, data was not stolen from the banks, and transactional systems, including the ATMs, remained untouched. The primary aim was disorienting service access among the customers through the disruption of the public websites. Such incidences have not been taken lightly in the case of safeguarding against similar incidents. According to the former CEO Brian Moynihan, the Bank of America initiated cybersecurity measures that provided protection from similar attacks. Financial institution customers often receive news of cyberattack incidents from the news outlets, which is more frustrating as the silence of the affected institution could indicate malice or involvement in the attack. Tariq (2018) outlined the reports by USA Today on Federal officials warning companies that hackers could have stolen more than 500 million financial records within the last 12 months of the report dated 2014. Such news could be disappointing for customers who learn about the incident for the first time from the news entity and not the affected financial institutions. Reactions could include panic withdrawals that would result in financial losses.

Cyberattacks have been random in different years, with the employed measures ineffective in resolving the situation. Tariq (2018) denoted the 2016 news reports on the targeted 46 major financial institutions through the distributed denial of service (DDoS). During the attack, the hackers were able to remotely control hundreds of computers and servers, which provided the gateway to flooding the targeted server with data and eliminate the possibility of obtaining an authentic traffic. NBC added that the targets included the New York Stock Exchange, PNC Banks, and Bank of America. The company most affected by the breach was JPMorgan, as data belonging to more than 83 million customers was stolen. Cyberattack incidents are also widespread in Europe. Tariq (2018) the several attack incidents in 2015 that took place online and affected online forex companies, including NASDAQ. Attacks in such platforms were characterized by initiation of transfers from various accounts. During these attacks, the authorities can apprehend the attackers in some incidences and are unsuccessful in others. Maitra (2015) outlined the 27th of January 2011 attacks where the UK police arrested the members of a group named Anonymous. The members of this group were linked to hacking a security firm and affecting the firm's clients, including Morgan Stanley and the Bank of America, and pushing for the WikiLeaks. The article noted that the aim of this group promoting a persistent non-violent campaign to ensure the 'power elite' stepped down and the disintegration of the 'Primary Dealers in the Federal Reserve banking system to bear the accountability for the disintegration of the World economy (Maitra 2015). The author noted that the Anonymous group orchestrated the DDoS attacks targeting companies providing WikiLeaks. Matra (2015) stated that with the presence of the Anonymous group on the internet and the availability of technology and hacking tools, Anonymous and other cyber-criminal groups could achieve everything without a physical presence in the targeted company.

In the various cyber-crime attack incidents, the victims, especially the attacked companies and corporations, downplayed the importance of communication as a means of mitigating the attack and resulting in additional losses. White (2021) observed that a cyberattack does not specifically result in physical destruction as it involves the disruption of a programs' ordinary functioning. These impacts denote the different panic generated from a cyberattack. The reaction type impacts the victims' panic and psychological well-being. Steingartner (2021) highlighted the importance of the continued evolution in security technologies as a means of equating to the transformation characterizing the business operating environment. Product managers need to resolve the new cyber risks and security challenges emanating from the developed infrastructures, business operating technologies, and security systems.

CYBERTERRORISM AND CYBERCRIME ON EDUCATIONAL INSTITUTIONS

The growing cyberattacks incidents targeting government and business corporations mean that educational institutions need to employ the right measures in strengthening their cybersecurity and reducing incidences that could compromise the quality of education and instruction in schools, colleges, and universities. Educational institutions encounter other major challenges such as inadequate resources, funding, and the teaching staff. However, these challenges do not reduce the instances of cyber-crime attacks. As a result, the educational institutions need to prioritize cybersecurity as it does to other arising needs. The cybersecurity concerns in academic institutions have been elicited by increasing reliance on computer systems and networks for communicating, exchanging, and storing academic information. Characteristically, these concerns have emanated from the growing use of e-learning systems. A significant research body has focused on e-learning, with minimal attention directed towards the security concerns from the new forms of learning. The educational institutions face unique challenges in ensuring the security of e-learning systems as they are accessed and controlled through the internet by thousands of individuals serving different capacities in the network. Levy et al. (2013) highlighted the minimal attention accorded to the severity of cyberattacks despite the importance of security issues to the information system. The internet could pose security challenges to the e-learning systems, including unauthorized access, acquiring sensitive information, and enabling academic misconduct.

45

The educational institutions encounter unique challenges that necessitate adopting cybersecurity measures to avoid worse case scenarios that would worsen the magnitude of the challenges. Levy et al. (2013) highlighted the Federal Bureau of Investigation (FBI) reports on a survey from 2006 organizations. The report highlighted those businesses incurred $67.2 billion annually in security expenditures. Some of these expenditures could be unattainable for most learning institutions, necessitating the adoption of cybersecurity measures to safeguard from the highlighted scenarios. The worrying thing about breaches in the learning institution is that the students' safety is compromised. The institutions have the mandate to safeguard the students and ensuring their safety, with some of these students being minors. The use of information systems has positively ensured effective and efficient learning while contributing to learning outcomes. E-learning systems are an essential aspect of information systems in educational institutions. Levy et al. (2013) stated that e-learning systems emanated from computer communication applications devised in the early 1980s. These systems have gone through significant growth in recent years, from higher education while slowly infusing into the government agencies and corporate organizations. Students and parents alike are embracing the e-learning system due to its convenience and ability to enable them to concentrate on other activities as they continue with their education. Levy et al. (2013) noted that by 2010, more than 5.6 million students in the United States had enrolled in at least a single online course. Online enrollment in colleges and universities has gone through drastic growth of at least 13% or 758,000 students annually in recent years. Characteristically, online learning makes up 32% of adult education.

Reliance on e-learning system does not apply solely in the provision of academic education. Levy et al. (2013) highlighted the inclusion of these systems in the delivery of various training modules, including medical, military, and corporate training. In medical education nurses and other medical practitioners are relying on the online e-learning system to acquire refresher courses and certificate training. On the other hand, businesses are opting to use e-learning systems to provide human resource training. The reliance on e-learning systems in the provision of education is not solely concentrated in western countries. However, these countries lead in the heavy reliance on the said learning systems. Alharthi et al. (2015) noted that reliance on e-learning systems is in its initial stages in developing countries such as those in the Arab region. The adoption and reliance on technologies in Arab countries compared to countries in Europe and North America is still in its early stages. Alharthi et al. (2015) outlined the e-learning system's growth in popularity in higher educational institutions while also being used to supplement technology for on-campus courses. Despite e-learning systems being a crucial element for ensuring learning and provision of training in organizational settings, these entities face the challenge of ensuring a secure learning environment. Levy et al. (2013) highlighted cyberattacks as having a crippling impact on e-learning systems in higher education institutions. These systems faced the threats imposed by reliance on information systems, which include unauthorized access, denial of services, hacking, and data alteration.

Online learning relies on the internet for execution, exposing the entire education system to the illegal activities and security threats prevailing over the internet. Chen and Wu (2013) observed that despite the illegal activities and security threats on the internet and which the e-learning environment is continually exposed to, many education institutions do not have the right frameworks to mitigate such challenges. The authors added that many educational institutions are rushing to adopt online learning without having a clearly articulated plan and an adequate understanding of the security process characterizing the online learning environment. Chen and Wu (2013) observed that in a recent survey undertaken by Campus Computing and WCET, the results denoted that 88% of the interviewed institutions had adopted a learning management system as a means of providing online courses. Adams and Blandford (2003), as cited by Chen and Wu (2013), stated that security in online learning involves the availability of learning resources and unimpaired to authorized users when the need arises. Online learning takes place through the internet, and every aspect of the learning process is a potential target of hacking or any other cyberattack. Chen and Wu (2013) observed that it is imperative for online learning to consider the security risks. The attention online learning system receives from cyber criminals who prosper on their ability to attack these systems. The authors articulated the increasing risks due to the growing complexities in the functionalities and characteristics of online learning systems. Cybersecurity is not limited to the educational environment and requires the collaboration of teachers, parents, and students. Parents should ensure the online safety of the children even when they are at home. Blackburn et al. (2019) observed that children these days use computers and other electronic devices at an early stage than they did in the past. The text highlighted that if an electronic device with a webcam is infected with Trojan or any other virus, hackers can easily obtain access and snap unauthorized pictures through the camera. Blackburn et al. (2019) added that most cases flagged by the police department are associated with face social media and morphed pictures. An additional threat is the revenge porn, where there is the release of explicit content to the internet without the owner's consent.

Students could be easily carried by the heat of the moment and end up compromising their sensitive information and the entire information system. Careless clicking on suspicious inks could easily lead a cyber-criminal to an information system in a learning institution. Blackburn et al. (2019) highlighted a tip at the Lakewood Crest High School that prompted the administration to locate more than 60 photos exchanged among students. The authors noted that the students shared the images through 'ghost apps' masquerading as calculators. The students entered a secret code that and the app provided a hidden screen containing images and videos. The institution expressed concern despite the sharing of the photos and videos taking place on the students' devices. The students may be lured to continue with the exchanges through computer systems in the school. The COVID-19 pandemic has interrupted learning processes, forcing many learning institutions to adopt online learning with adequate preparation for the same. The increasing remote learning is increasing vulnerability to more cyberattacks, and there is no sign of the risks dwindling with the schools having a back-to-back learning and heavily reliant on the internet for learning and accessing learning materials. Querolo and Singh (2021) highlighted the drastic increase in the number of cyberattacks in schools that have been publicly reported. The number of these incidents escalated to 408 in 2020 from 2016, as highlighted by K-12 Security Information Exchange. This organization oversees similar incidents. The highlighted number is not a true reflection of the cyberattack incidents targeting schools as most of them go unreported, with institutions fearing the backlash of parents, litigation, and panic student transfers. The high number could be attributed to the institutions' reluctance in ensuring cybersecurity. On the other hand, schools could be having the right protection policies, and the teaching staff and students may be circumventing the cybersecurity protections. Schools should avail necessary resources and employing the right restrictions to ensure that the users of the information systems know what is expected of them.

Education venues vary in size and purpose which translate to the different purpose of cyberattacks. These differences have been evidenced in the way these institutions deal with cyberattacks. Tidy (2021) observed that the Harris Federation had temporarily disabled emails as it deals with cyberattacks. This federation oversees 50 primary and secondary schools in and around London. During the attack, the data from the systems were encrypted and concealed by the attackers. When coming public about the attack, a statement from the Harris Federation website noted that the attack was at the fourth multi-academy trust. The attack was highly complex and significantly impacted the academies. The statement also acknowledged that the federation would take considerable time before fully unveiling in-depth details about the attack (Tidy 2021). In addition to disabling the emails, the Harris Federation had also disabled any devices which had been given to students. Querolo and Singh (2021) observed the increasing frequency of hacks in school systems of more than two attacks in every school day in 2020. This trend worried school officials due to the possibility of identity theft, increasing the costs of insurance against attacks and repairs following data breaches. The numerous cybercrimes that have hit K-12 schools during the pandemic have elicited concerns, especially among investors. Querolo and Singh (2021) stated that the Wall Street and people who have lent close to $600 billion to school districts in the bond market are concerned about the under controlled risks facing their investment.

Public schools struggling with cash challenges are potential targets of hackers targeting to obtain data, extort money, or even cause chaos in the wake of the surging cyberattacks. Hackers could be individuals that schools could rarely suspect. Querolo and Singh (2021) highlighted the alleged claims of a mother hacking a school to obtain a position for her daughter in a homecoming court. Compared to businesses and corporate organizations, schools have weaker cyber defense mechanisms to the minimal investment in in-house expertise. Attacks are increasing because they are cheaper to execute. Patterson (2021) highlighted ransomware as the new threat facing schools in the wake of the COVID-19 pandemic. For the K-12 schools that are the top target, the average ransoms are close to $50,000, while the top payments have reached $1.4 million. The article noted that according to the FBI, schools are the current popular targets for ransomware. Several factors contribute to schools being a preferred target for ransomware attacks. Patterson (2021) stated that according to IBM, educators and students lack adequate training on handling cyberattacks coupled by the modest school funding to mitigate attacks. Most educators claim that they rely on remote and virtual learning tools, with 60% of the teachers claiming that they have not received additional training on virtual training during the pandemic. Patterson 92021) observed that most teachers receive minimal technical support to foster their interaction with information systems. The FBI stated that hackers and cybercriminals are targeting schools with tools and strategies that were initially effective. The article cited the example of the ZeuS trojan, a malware targeting Microsoft Windows machines running on the school computer. This malware sends stolen data to criminals' servers and holds it hostage to blackmail the institutions for ransom or sell it on the dark web.

Cyberattacks targeting learning institutions have gone through significant changes over the years and are becoming more complex with increased remote learning. Students are among individuals charged for involvement in unauthorized access to computer systems. Finley (2011) stated that on 9th July 2008a student from Georgia Highlands College was charged with hacking a computer system, altering grades, and stealing passwords belonging to other teachers and students. Police authorities claimed that the student, Christopher Fowler used the login credentials of one of the professors at the school to access the institution's computer network. It was alleged that the student also hacked the Voice Over Internet Protocol (VoIP). There has been an increased reliance on wireless networks. Finley (2011) stated that 60.1% of public universities, 70% of private research universities, and 45% of community colleges have wireless networks. The Campus Computing Project oversees conducting research and providing data on information technology (IT) on U.S colleges and Educational Security Incidents (ESI). The provided education on cybersecurity to personnel could be inadequate or inefficient. Park et al. (2017) noted that despite fundamental security ethics education being provided at public institutions, the security technology education curriculums for the working-level security employees are inefficient due to inadequate security manpower, trainers, educational entities, and teaching aids. Also, most security personnel do not have much experience in practicing cyberattacks and may not comprehend attack patterns and could experience challenges when some systems are hacked. The training could be ineffective when employees in learning institutions are deliberately involved in cyberattacks. Finley (2011) observed that university employees are guilty of 47% of cyber-related incidents occurring in institutions, with the statistics bypassing the number of attacks conducted by hackers.

Cyber-crimes targeting the education sector primarily focused on the confiscation of information as these institutions are a harbor of loads of sensitive information belonging to the students, teachers, and even parents. Finley (2011) noted that the common cyber-related incidences in colleges and universities involve the release of information to unauthorized individuals. This information is often obtained from the university IT personnel. The number of reported cyber-related incidents rose by 67.5% to 139 incidents in 2007 and affected 112 college campuses in the United States. The physical pilferage of personal computers is also on the rise. There were 17.1% of reports on physical theft of personal computers, which had increased from 13.5% in 2005. Human factors play an instrumental role in the surging cyberattack incidents in the education sector. Misra and Adewumi (2019) highlighted the human factors as narrowing down to the interaction people have with tasks, technologies, and the environment to better understand and evaluate their interconnections. Social media is also another avenue creating vulnerabilities for computer systems and networks in education institutions. Reinforcing the human factor in social media situations requires the provision of education for students. This education should be provided at an early age when students are exposed to the world and the internet. Misra and Adewumi (2019) highlighted some of the cybersecurity approaches in training and mentorship as including interactive video learning. However, there should be adequate efforts to include scientific means of assisting humans in making minimal errors while avoiding being cyber-crime victims. Boring (2018) stipulated that despite computer technologies providing a significant aspect of security breaches, human errors involved in the attack are the primary weakness in the computer technologies are the primary weakness of computer security. The authors noted that human errors are responsible for 65% of incidents of security breaches. One of the prominent arguments is the human involvement in designing these systems, any loophole that leads to users making mistakes are human errors.

Decision-based errors occur when people make poor decisions due to a lack of information about a particular action or task. Human mistakes can occur due to people being fatigued, not paying enough attention, being distracted, or lack of awareness. Boring (2018) observed that policies put in an organization are not strenuous to follow but very important in ensuring some form of protection against cyberattacks. Some of the common human errors include.

➢ Using weak passwords or keeping passwords in untrustworthy locations, such as plain text or sticky notes on the workplace desk.

➢ Poor management of sensitive data: losing sensitive files by accident, without realizing they are essential, transmitting sensitive material to the incorrect people, and failing to back up important data are all examples of improper handling of sensitive data.

The highlighted errors are manageable through the provision of training and education on the importance of upholding measures to curb cyberattacks. An institution could enforce stringent measures such as a password system requiring strong passwords and multifactor authentication techniques such as biometric methods.

Dr. Tunde Alaofin

CYBERTERRORISM AND CYBERCRIME ON HEALTHCARE INSTITUTIONS

In the modern world, technology is transforming the globe's terrain and moving us toward a more sophisticated technological world. Information and communication technologies' (ICT) growing position in healthcare has had a significant influence. It improves medical quality, promotes patient security and data security, and lowers operational and administrative costs. In developed and developing countries, individuals and communities can benefit from improved health care due to information communication technologies (ICT). These technologies could help ICTs can help close in the information divides arising in the health sector in developing and new industrial countries—between health professionals and the communities they serve, and between the producers of health research and the needy practitioners. This gap could be resolved by providing new and more efficient ways of access, communication, and information storage. ICTs also give the position to foster health system efficiencies and reduce medical errors through the development of databases and other applications. Gole et al. (2017) observed that the increased use of ICT in healthcare is a prerequisite for developing, deploying, and creating new healthcare technology.

The evolving technologies and their reliance on the provision of healthcare services have fostered some services that would be impossible in traditional settings. A medical practitioner in a distant rural hospital is initially unable to provide a diagnosis when faced with a patient who exhibits a wide range of symptoms. However, by using the hospital's Internet connection, he can diagnose and provide feasible treatment options. Research has been delved into improving the reliance on ICT in providing better medical assistance. Gole et al. (2017) highlighted that the Committee on Quality of Health Care in America and Institute of Medicine in 2001 examined how the healthcare system may be renewed to encourage innovation and improve service delivery. This agency aspires to provide safe, equitable, patient-centered, effective, efficient, and timely health care. On the issue of incorporating ICT in healthcare, the bone of contention is providing healthcare services to the masses in an efficient and cost-effective manner. This necessitates infrastructure improvement to enable the adoption of cutting-edge technology to improve service delivery efficacy in terms of cost, time, and reach. Health information systems (HIS) have been a crucial aspect of infusing ICT in the healthcare sector. A HIS is a system that consolidates data collecting, processing, reporting, and utilization of information to improve healthcare effectiveness and efficiency through improved management at all levels. Gavurová et al. (2018) stated that a HIS in a healthcare facility could be a beneficial tool for determining how to deal with an increasing number of patients. It provides for the management of operations such as admissions and transfers, laboratory test results, and so on. The hospital's information system may help reduce the amount of work required and, as a result, the expenses associated with these procedures. Due to the many different producers of healthcare information systems, massive data analysis must cope with the variances in system and database architecture (Gavurová et al., 2018).

The role played by these health care information systems creates vulnerabilities that increase the possibility of cyberattacks. Gavurová et al. (2018) highlighted that healthcare professionals employ information and communication technologies to ease the electronic recording, storage, and sharing of various forms of patient data. It could be used to diagnose diseases at an early stage, manage individual and population health, and more effectively detect healthcare fraud. These functions are detrimental, making the health sector a preferred target by cyber criminals. Alimbaev et al. (2021) observed that the reliance on modern ICT in healthcare has been necessitated by massive information as well as technologies for gathering, analyzing, and sharing data. Some of the prominent health information systems include e-health that yields electronic health records (EHR). A lot of processes characterize electronic health (e-health) and its inclusion in healthcare. Churi et al. (2021) observed that in e-health, most advanced technologies are incorporated into medical infrastructures, including extensive monitoring and transfer of health-related concerns from the patient-concerned environment to the appropriate service provider.

In the healthcare industry, the amount of data created is continually increasing. The features of e-health systems increase the potential of cyberattacks. The article outlined the 2012 IBM global business services executive report that denoted the entire healthcare system as shifting from a disease-centered to a patient-centered model. The yielded EHRs are the assessments and analyses carried out in accordance with the illnesses. Kwiatkowska et al. (2016) defined EHR as the patient's longer-term electronic record, which consists of or is entirely made up of data from many Electronic Medical Records (EMR) and Electronic Patient Records (EPR). This record is shared and transferred across the healthcare system and between institutions that provide healthcare services. Patient-centeredness is also a feature of EHR.

OECD (2016), as cited by Kwiatkowska et al. (2016), stated that the goal of EHR is to compile a patient's contact history with healthcare providers from various organizations that provide care to the individual. EHR provides a real-time record. It also enables secure and immediate access to patient information. Considering the massive sensitive information characterizing the healthcare sector, healthcare cybersecurity has emerged as one of the significant risks in healthcare. IT workers must constantly handle healthcare data security challenges. The handling of health cybersecurity and electronic health records should align with the ethical obligation to assist patients and mitigate the dangers that healthcare security breaches might pose to their lives. EHRs have lots of sensitive information on patients' medical history, making hospital cybersecurity a top IT priority. Physicians and other healthcare workers, as well as insurance companies, can communicate vital information through EHRs. This makes it easy to organize care as well as deal with insurance issues. In traditional healthcare settings, it was impossible for medical professionals to interact in such dynamic ways to fulfill the needs of patients. Hunter (2013) voiced that suitable privacy and security safeguards must be built into the electronic record system from the start. The article outlined that the Office of the National Coordinator for Health Information Technology, which is a section of the U.S. Department of Health and Human Services, has a cybersecurity checklist with advice on how to avoid data security and confidentiality breaches.

Lots of advantages are attributed to the use of EHR in the provision of healthcare services. However, the disadvantages of potential cyberattack reduce these systems' effectiveness and potentially increase more harm due to the possibility of patients' medical history being stolen and shared with unauthorized individuals. Chenthara et al. (2019) pointed out that recently, EHR in healthcare has encountered issues with privacy breaches and unauthorized access to medical records, the most serious of which is related to privacy and security of medical data. Some of the cybersecurity issues affecting EHR include malware attacks that impair the integrity of systems and endanger patient confidentiality, while distributed denial-of-service (DDoS) assaults can impede a facility's ability to deliver patient care. In healthcare settings, cyberattacks like Ransomware can have far-reaching consequences beyond financial loss and data leak. Hackers hacked into Community Health Systems (CHS) databases earlier this year, which is one of the largest hospital groups in the United States. Chenthara et al. (2019) noted that the attack resulted in the access of 4.5 million patients' personal health information, names, addresses, and personal data, including social security numbers. As part of their hacktivism, hackers from the Internet vigilante group Anonymous targeted multiple hospitals, unleashing a DDoS attack on the hospital's website. As a result, protecting the privacy, security, confidentiality, integrity, and availability of protected health information (PHI) in electronic health records (EHR) is a necessity for the healthcare system to ensure utmost discharging of its mandate, which is the patients' health and wellbeing (Chenthara et al. 2019). Unauthorized access to the health system and its impact on social, economic, political, and cultural disputes necessitate the highest level of cyber security.

Cybersecurity breaches are criminal incidents due to unauthorized access and utilization of patients' information and defiance of stipulated rules and regulations on handling patients' data. Koczkodaj et al. (2019) observed that under the Health Insurance Portability and Accountability Act, a breach refers to the unlawful acquisition, access, use, or disclosure of protected health information (PHI) that jeopardizes the security or privacy of such data. The data analyzed by the article articulated that since the EHR data was first collected in October, 173 million entries have been compromised. One-third of the US population might have been affected by the data beaches. It is paramount to note that numerous criminals may have used the same EHRs. Besides the increasing reliance on information systems in the provision of the healthcare system, these institutions boast of holding massive data, a catch point for infusing ransomware and identity theft. Koczkodaj et al. (2019) voiced that cyberattacks resulted in the exposure of more than 11 million healthcare records in June 2016. Indeed, the healthcare industry was responsible for the top three data security breaches. The 'Health Warning' report by the Intel Security McAfee Labs articulated that health care data is exploited and monetized by cybercriminals with more time and resources. Particularly, perpetrators' behaviors are becoming increasingly aggressive. After stealing medical records, criminals must examine the information and cross-check it with information from other sources before identifying chances of enticing fraud, data/identity theft, extortion, and blackmail. HHS Breach Portal (2017), as cited by Koczkodaj et al. (2019), noted that the amount of security data breaches reported by the U.S government's Health and Human Services Agency has been published online.

Cyberattacks are primarily capitalizing on the vulnerabilities and concerns arising in the use of electronic health records. Fatima et al. (2020) observed that according to a survey of primary care physicians in the United States, most doctors believed that electronic health records are beneficial. However, in the responses by these practitioners, privacy, and secrecy of eHealth services were cited as a major concern. According to a study on the influence of health disclosure laws on health information exchanges. The presence of secure privacy and confidentiality rules that limit the publication of health information data led to more significant health information exchanges across healthcare institutions. Other research studies examined individual perceptions towards electronic health records and found that the discerned effectiveness of regulatory mechanisms and the perceived effectiveness of technological mechanisms both had a positive impact on trust, with technological mechanisms positively impacting perceived privacy control and trust. Lots of challenges could be associated with the electronic health records being obtained by cybercriminals. Users of electronic medical records may face substantial financial, social, and psychological difficulties if sensitive information and other factors of health informatics acceptance and diffusion are revealed to unauthorized individuals. Different countries encounter different challenges and security concerns in their implementation of electronic health records. Fatima et al. (2020) informed of the study on Dubai's privacy perception and privacy protection regulations in the years 2015–2016 prior to the EMR implementation at the Dubai Health Authority (DHA). In the study, most survey respondents in Dubai trusted eHealthcare services and did not believe their data privacy and confidentiality were in jeopardy.

The shortcomings of the electronic health records system increase vulnerabilities to cyberattacks. According to Chenthara et al. (2020, the existing approach has a major flaw in that healthcare records are held in centralized systems in silos, making healthcare data a particularly appealing target for hackers. Several studies have found that centralization increases security concerns and necessitates reliance on a single authority. Due to centralized databases, healthcare systems are subject to attacks that escalate into cyber threats, such as the recent Ransomware attack and the Equifax attack, which compromise the privacy and security of EHRs. Another major issue confronting the healthcare business today is the lack of interoperability in electronic health records (EHR). Due to varied formats and standards, health data in current systems is disintegrated and challenging to communicate with healthcare practitioners or stakeholders. The individual aspects of EHR elicit concerns for healthcare practitioners, and which could be easily manipulated. Chentahra et al. (2020) added that internal assaults, in which employees with authorized credentials within businesses access data, such as database administrators or key managers, are a serious risk for health records stored on cloud servers and are far worse than external attacks.

Furthermore, if the EHR is removed from the hospital's database, the record may be permanently lost, which is another concern that deserves careful consideration. It is imperative for healthcare systems to have a tamper-proof system, only accessible to authorized individuals. To protect patient privacy, limited access to patient records to specific physicians, laboratories, and pharmacies is preferable to full public access. Furthermore, because health records are controlled by service providers, people do not have complete authority over them under the current system. Secure storage and scalability of medical records are important concerns as healthcare data continues to grow.

Given the sensitivity of healthcare data, efficient data exchange among stakeholders in the public domain is a complex undertaking. Despite the unique features provided by the current healthcare business, it lacks an efficient means to store, share, and analyze health data in a global uniform manner. The current privacy-preserving techniques are insufficient to assure perfect security for cloud-based EHR management. Phishing is one of the security concerns in electronic health records. Mohamed (2020) stated that Phishing is an internet cybercrime in which a cybercriminal targets a regular computer or mobile phone user via email. This interaction is primarily intended to entice users to divulge sensitive information such as personal health records, bank account information, and passwords. The attacker sends an email impersonating a reputable company or individual in a phishing assault. To persuade the recipient to click on a questionable link, the cybercriminal employs social engineering techniques. The link might either download a malicious program or direct the user to a form where they must submit sensitive personal information. In healthcare settings, phishing attacks could target patients, medical practitioners, and hospital employees. Various factors motivate the attackers, including monetary gain or establishing a name in the cybercriminal world. A stolen personal health care record might be sold for thousands of dollars. According to a recent IBM Security research, the healthcare industry has the highest average cost of a data breach (Mohamed 2020). According to the study, phishing is one of the most prevalent tactics for launching an assault. In the United States, around 15 million patient records were compromised in 2018.

Furthermore, 25 million patients were affected in the first six months of 2019, with phishing being the primary cause of most breaches. Phishing not only has a devastating impact on people's financial holdings, but it also creates doubt every time they are approached via text or email. Individuals' trust on electronic media to perform a variety of activities is shattered due to phishing. This situation jeopardizes the digitization of traditional paper-based patient data.

Internet of Things (IoT) is another healthcare system that could be a potential target by cybercriminals. Hussain et al. (2021) stated that IoT is a communication paradigm creating a connection and interaction among devices. In an IoT-based healthcare system and due to data being directly tied to humans, security is a top priority. An intensive care unit (ICU) is a special and crucially operable department of a hospital where patients who require essential medical care receive specialized treatment. In protecting patients' privacy, some systems use fog computing to do some of the computation on the edge, rather than sending identifiable information to the cloud. Hussain et al. (2021) noted that cyber-intruders narrow down to IoT healthcare systems when conducting cyberattacks. The authors reported that more than 90% of cyberattacks have been the point of focus in cyberattacks. The healthcare industry has become attractive to cyber-criminals, according to the 2017 White House intelligence reports.

Furthermore, throughout the COVID-19 era, cyberattacks increased rapidly as COVID-19 expanded. Cybercriminals have been actively attacking IoT healthcare services and infrastructure. The safety of the healthcare system is detrimental to the patients' health and recovery. Hussain et al. (2021) detailed that in IoT healthcare environments, the confidentiality and integrity of data are critical. Any data breach or interference in healthcare systems might expose patients to major health risks. Similarly, any modification to the patient's medical record that goes unnoticed by the professional medical staff could result in unintentional death. Characteristically, cyberattacks on IoT healthcare systems have the potential to seriously interrupt medical procedures. For instance, if a hacker gains access to an infusion pump and modifies its configuration so that it begins releasing a high amount of insulin to a patient, resulting in severe hypoglycemia. There could be cases where a cybercriminal gains access to a pacemaker and either slows or speeds up the heartbeat. Hussain et al. (2021) observed that following such attacks, the patient may experience severe bradycardia or tachycardia, which can result in mortality. As a result, the security of healthcare systems has become the most pressing issue of our day.

The Internet of Medical Things (IoMT) is another healthcare system constantly encountering cyberterrorism and cyberattack threats. Rose et al. (2020) defined IoMT as devices connecting to healthcare IT systems through network connections that are becoming more common, especially in hospitals, patients, and medical professionals who use connected devices for routine medical processes. The article highlighted that the IoMT was anticipated to have 3.7 million devices in 2018, with the market expected to reach USD 136.8 billion by 2021. Rose et al. (2020) noted that one of the advantages of IoMT linked devices is that they can provide real-time information about a patient's condition via the internet, and patients do not need to go to an emergency room or a hospital. These devices are used to monitor heart rate and blood pressure at the bedside where devices such as pacemakers and insulin delivery systems, for example, can be programmed to fulfill functions automatically or even connect to a doctor's computer to allow medical workers to monitor or treat a patient.

CYBERTERRORISM AND CYBERCRIME
ON REAL-LIFE EXAMPLES

Individuals with no affiliations to education, government, corporation, or health institutions have been victims of cyberterrorism and cyberattacks due to vulnerabilities in personal computers and mobile devices and their use of social media platforms. Terrorist organizations and their supporters are increasingly using the Internet for various purposes, including recruitment, financing, incitement to commit terrorist acts, and the gathering and dissemination of information for terrorist purposes, thanks to technological advancements. Cyberterrorism targeting individuals could aim at sending a message to their given country. As the computer has become vital to commerce, entertainment, and government, cybercrime has grown in importance, particularly through the Internet. One of the most crucial aspects of cybercrime is its non-local characteristic, with acts occurring in regions separated by vast distances. The non-localized aspect of cybercrimes presents significant challenges for law enforcement since local or even national crimes increasingly necessitate worldwide cooperation. Leukfeldt et al. (2017) observed that one crucial issue is that cybercrime is a complex subject to grasp. Cybercrimes cover a wide range of crimes; some are motivated by economic considerations, while others are motivated by philosophy, passion, or even retribution. In the convergence of cyberspace and terrorism, cyberterrorism could result in the intimidation of some individuals.

Human interaction is creating avenues for cybercrimes, especially through internet forums and technological devices. Wilcox and Bhattacharya (2020) highlighted social engineering as a crucial human aspect enabling hacking while using social media. The authors decried the obscured differentiation between social and organizational interactions following the introduction of social media in various forms in organizations. Traditional security solutions are falling behind as more firms experience intrusions narrowing down to human aspects such as social engineering. Wilcox and Bhattacharya (2020) noted that most employees have a natural tendency to trust others and share information in a helpful, well-intentioned manner. Social engineers make use of these human tendencies to launch an attack from the outside, allowing them to obtain unnoticed access to the company's most secure sections for their own nefarious purposes. Due to the nature of social networking, people are encouraged to trust and connect with their communities. These tendencies create a vulnerability exploited by cybercriminals. Cybercriminals looking to prey on victims can easily take advantage of this trust (Wilcox & Bhattacharya 2020). In the wake of the increased cyber-crimes through social media, efforts could include a holistic security framework encompassing technological, procedural, and user-centric controls, as well as process advice for businesses adopting ever-evolving technologies like social media adoption. The article noted that social media rules and guidelines provide necessary guidance on how to apply social media involvement to all members of an organization. Such efforts could eliminate the individual social media attacks that could trickle to the organization.

Identity theft is one of the cyber-crimes affecting social media users at a personal level. Tidy (2021) questioned the amount of data people willingly share through social media platforms. This information could include name, location, marital status, and age. The article highlighted the compilation of data acquired from 700 million LinkedIn users globally, which was up for sale at $5,000. Tidy (2021) stated that the incident and other comparable instances of social network scraping, have prompted a heated debate over whether the fundamental personal information we provide openly on social media profiles should be better protected. The involved hacker, Tom Liner, provided a link to a million-record sample, as well as an invitation for other hackers to contact him privately and make offers for his database. The news of the LinkedIn scrapping incident sparked debate in the cyber-security and privacy communities about whether people should be concerned about the increasing cases of mega-scrapes. It is worth noting that the databases formed by cybercriminals are not formed by gaining access to social network servers or websites. Instead, they are mostly built by scraping the public-facing surface of platforms with automated programs to extract whatever information about users is openly available (Tidy 2021). Stolen and consolidated data could be formed by just going through each social network profile page one at a time. However, gathering as much data as the hackers are capable of would take numerous lifetimes.

In the year 2021, there have been several incidents of 'scraping' social media pages. Tidy (2021) stated that in April, a hacker sold a database of 500 million records scraped from LinkedIn. In the week of the first incident, another hacker posted a database on a free forum the scraped information obtained from 1.3 million Clubhouse profiles. In a third incident in the same month of APRIL, 533 million Facebook user information was consolidated from a combination of old and modern scraping before being given free on a hacker forum with a request for donations. The hacks on social media platforms have targeted users that are influential in various capacities. Potkin (2020) highlighted the Twitter hack that jeopardized notable people's accounts, including US presidential contender Joe Biden, reality TV star Kim Kardashian, and former US President Barack Obama as one of the most pronounced social media ages. The incident was not the first, as it joined the list of some of the most well-known cyberattacks and security breaches to have hit social media companies. Twitter, the company, highlighted that the hack came after employees with access to the company's internal systems were jeopardized, and hackers "used their access to take over several highly visible and verified accounts. Potkin (2020) noted that it was not the first time the Titter employees were a target. The U.S government highlighted that in November 2019, two former Twitter employees were charged for spying on behalf of Saudi Arabia and gaining access to information on renegades who use the network.

Social media and the information provided on these platforms provide the leeway for identity theft. In keeping in touch with individuals one knows, social media may be a fun and valuable tool. However, the bone of contention is the safety of the provided personal information. Equifax (2021) highlighted social media as playing an instrumental role in the high incidences of identity fraud in 2016. Identity thieves could extract personal information from social media profiles or postings to conduct crimes, depending on how much you disclose online and an individual's privacy settings. Cybercrimes could include utilizing of personal information to send scam emails or credit, driver's licenses, or passports applications. Someone may even mimic you on dating websites by using your social media profile photo and location. Equifax (2021) outlined the variations in the details shared on social media profiles depending on platform on use. The article highlighted Twitter's restriction on the amount of shared information. Resolving the cybercrimes requires the collaborative effort between the government, social media companies, and social media users. However, there are basic measures social media users could take in preventing identity theft or any other cybercrimes that could compromise their safety. The first thong would be to avoid sharing information or documents containing personal details. One may feel the need to share documents such as an acceptance letter, a paid credit card bill, or a letter from a new job offer. Equifax (2021) highlighted the importance of checking privacy settings before sharing personal information. The privacy settings should be set that only trusted individuals can view the personal information.

Answering security questions is a requirement for most social networking sites. Some of the required personal data include phone numbers, emails, and areas of residency. The North Country Savings Bank (2021) stated that while this information may appear non-essential, it can be quite hazardous in the hands of an identity thief. This information could include one's favorite color or where one went to high school, which are featured as common security questions for financial accounts. Social media users often feel the need to share information, such as visiting fancy hotels and restaurants. According to the North Country Savings Bank (2021), sharing such visits notifies individuals that one is not at home, making one vulnerable to crime while also revealing sensitive information about locations one frequents. The article highlighted the importance of turning off geotags on posts, especially on sites such as Facebook and Instagram, which turn on them by default, making it easier for hackers to trace locations when one makes posts or upload photos. Equifax (2021) sensitized verification that the people one connects with on social media are who they claim they are. You can get a request to connect from someone you know, but it could be a scammer impersonating them. If one can, it is crucial to try to verify their identification offline.

Dr. Tunde Alaofin

CRIPPLING AND DESTRUCTION OF NETWORKS, SYSTEMS, AND CITIZENS

Networks

Many nations consider cyberterrorism to be a top-tier national concern because of the possible harm and disruption it might bring due to the world's increasing reliance on IT infrastructure. While governments, banks, and utilities such as the communication infrastructure, water, oil, and gas are obvious targets, Cyberterrorism groups are becoming more organized and complex in their attacks and will make utmost effort to cause economic, political, physical disaster and destroy critical national infrastructure. As a result, Cyberterrorism impacts everyone, from huge corporations to ordinary people who possess or use a computer connected to the Internet. Cyberterrorism is not the first instance that new technology has been exploited as a strategic flaw. Cyberterrorists could potentially use the Internet to steal credit card details or other vital information to fund their operations. Cyberterrorism has gotten a lot of press, although it has mostly been used for propaganda or information gathering. Nevertheless, cyberterrorism and cyberattacks have significantly crippled and destroyed computer networks. A computer network refers to a group of computers linked together so that one computer to foster communication with another and sharing of data, resources, and applications. In the networks, computers could be connected through cables or have a wireless connection for the purpose of the data and resources exchange. In differentiating computer networks from other networks, Peterson and Davie (2012) highlighted the key aspect as being generality. The authors highlighted

71

computer networks as built for general reasons for programmable hardware as opposed to being optimized for a specific application, including making phone calls. Some of the commonly used computer networks include the local area network (LAN), wireless local area network (WLAN), and wide area network (WAN).

The modern computer networks are increasingly taking over functions that were undertaken by single networks in the past. Luo (2010) noted that computer network technology has gradually become a fundamental component of society, business, and life in the setting of big data. The computer network allows data to be instantly transferred and shared, making people's life easier. Guo (2021) added that libraries have widely employed computer networks to replace traditional office procedures in the information era. The computer networks' popularity has enhanced the library's management and office efficiency and has also offered readers more convenient service options. However, suppose there is an issue with the network, which is the high openness. In that case, it means that a lot of information containing viruses is randomly dispersed in the network, posing a significant concealed threat to computer network security. The normal development of the library business office and reader services in computer networks would be hampered by concealed security dangers in the computer network. Simultaneously, it will have a negative impact on the development and usage of digital resources in libraries, as well as readers' enthusiasm for using library resources. Wang et al. (2020) attributed the developing society to the drastic advancements in network technology. Computer network technology is associated with various aspects of the internet, which translates to increased vulnerabilities, cyberterrorism, and cyberattack incidents.

Thencreased reliance on computer networks elicits conversations on aspects such as network security and the adverse impact of cyberattacks on these networks and the involved data and individuals. Huang (2021) noted that the current computer networks have made a reality the notion of the closeness of the ends of the earth. In recent years, human life has been so connected to the internet, which elicits the possibility of adverse cyberattacks targeting computer systems. Because 90% of the world's population wants to use the Internet, the issue of network security is growing more relevant. Huang (2021) stated that with the rise in popularity of big data, the value of data is putting a greater emphasis on network security. Virus attacks and hacker activities have significantly impacted the normal order of network society and national security. As a result, in the current era, computer network security protection is critical. Luo (2020) observed that conventional network security challenges such as network viruses, hacker attacks, and vulnerabilities of network system are not the only dangers to computer network security. Big data and cloud computing have created a slew of new risks that are continually changing. As a result, computer network security technology is becoming increasingly important.

Computer network security is an adverse subject whose examination is imperative in determining the impact of cyberattacks and cyberterrorism. Wang and Liu (2021) noted that hardware, software, resources, and other security are all included in computer network security. As a result, ensuring the security of a computer network entails ensuring the security of computer hardware, software, resources to avoid their destruction or leakage, as well as having an impact on the computer network system's operation. While considering the situation, it is imperative to take adequate preventive measures and procedures to protect the security of information and the orderly progress of relevant activity. Computer network security is a form of security preservation for a developed technology employed in some processing systems to safeguard the software and hardware computer data from being leaked and destroyed due to unanticipated circumstances. He (2021) defined network security as the maintenance of the integrity and availability of information on the internet. Integrity refers to the ability to prevent unauthorized operations from altering data. Effectiveness refers to the ability to prevent unauthorized actions from destroying data or computer resources. As a result, network security and information security are two primary aspects of network system security. He (2021) noted that network security involves the security of physical lines and connections associated with network operation and interconnections in the operating system, networks, and the security of personnel management. On the other hand, information security involves data security while factoring in the data's availability, confidentiality, and authenticity.

The several factors affecting computer network security could have a direct and indirect association with cyberterrorism and cyberattacks. Chui (2019) highlighted illegal invasion as one of the aspects challenging computer network security. When undertaking network operations, the computer is frequently exposed to the potential of illegal intrusion, which compromises data confidentiality and integrity. Network hackers employ monitoring to unlawfully capture IP packets, data messages, passwords, or usernames from the computer network. The acquired details are then used to enter the computer network to illegally steal, tamper with, or erase data information from the IP address on the machine as a computer user. Chui (2019) highlighted leakage of network server information as a problem faced by computer network security. The article noted that the computer operating system, which requires professional compilation, still has flaws. For network hacking, professional computer theory and expert computer network operation abilities are required. As a result, they frequently use computer system flaws to launch network assaults on computers, illegally collecting network data and posing a severe threat to computer network security.

Chui (2019) outlined that the computer virus is another challenge to computer network security. Computer viruses are diverse, extensively spread, and highly contagious, impacting other host devices in the computer network system to varying degrees. In the worst-case scenario, viruses threaten to bring the entire computer network system to a halt. Most computer viruses are kept in applications. Suppose the cleaning and scanning of the virus is not undertaken in due time. In that case, the opening of the file containing the virus could result in its activation and immediately spread and infect other devices. Network defects is another problem of computer network security. According to Chui (2019), a running computer operating system often supports several processes or users simultaneously, and the host of a computer network system allows multiple users to connect simultaneously. When the system sends or gets data, all processes or users who are active at the same moment may be required to send or receive data. Once a computer's network has a flaw, hackers can easily target it, making data and information security impossible to ensure. As a result, relevant people must devote their whole attention to it. Wang et al. (2020) highlighted network vulnerabilities as a computer security risk that facilitates hacking and makes computers more susceptible to malware infestation. This weakness is especially true for some users who make no attempt at network security, posing a major threat to network computer security.

Network security protection is an important effort of derailing cyberattacks while safeguarding from the adverse effects associated with the same. Jiang (2021) outlined reliance on independent security protection to boost the security of a network system by using. These efforts increase the technological challenge of independent security protection. Viruses, worms, botnets, and other forms of information security assaults have increasingly progressed in the direction of integration, which is also gradually expanding towards being complex and diverse. Following the continued rise of network attacks, criminals are gradually exploiting hosts' software and hardware vulnerabilities, forming a chain of network attacks in the black industry. New attack methods are evolving because of the utilization of information technology, posing several security risks. Therefore, it is imperative to innovate information security technologies in the information network environment as a means of improving host security protection. Huo (2019) recognized the complexity of creating network security and noted that the key to ensuring network information security is to develop a comprehensive network information security system. Efforts by foreign and local scholars included the utilization of different approaches to assess network security, which have achieved significant progress, which mostly includes the development of the hierarchical structure model of computer network security evaluation, and the fuzzy analytic hierarchy process based on the triangular fuzzy number to determine the quantitative evaluation aspects of the computer network security.

Cyberattacks and cyberterrorism destroy computer networks in many ways. These tactics end up crippling the computer networks and compromising the exchanged data. An example of a cyberattack technique is the advanced persistent threat (APT). Feras (2020) noted that the phrase "advanced persistent threat" (APT) usually refers to a series of well-coordinated and persistent attacks on computer networks by hackers or cybercriminals to acquire valuable data from businesses. Gregory Rattray, an Air Force Colonel in the United States, is associated with APT. Rattray developed the term to describe data-exfiltration Trojans aimed at taking advantage of shortcomings in computer networks. In theory, an APT is a broad phrase that refers to a set of long-term, clandestine, and persistent cyberattacks aimed at obtaining valuable data for industrial espionage or political action from organizations, states, or corporations.

Friedberg et al. (2015), as cited by Feras (2020), defined APT as a slow-moving cyberattack with the goal of gaining unauthorized access by surreptitiously compromising the security of networked information systems. Initially, an APT strives to acquire access to a system, but the long-term goal is to spread across the network to steal legal papers, intellectual property, and other critical information. Tankard (2011), as cited by Feras (2020), highlighted APT as a new form of insidious threats used to carry out a series of stealthy and undetectable attacks against computer networks or systems over an extended period. Advanced vectors or tactics are used to acquire access, and the threats last for a long time. The article outlined the United States National Institute of Standards and Technology (NIST) as proposing one of the widely used APT definitions. NIST highlighted APT as an adversary with advanced levels of competence and substantial resources that allow it to create opportunities to achieve its goals by employing many attack vectors. As denoted by the report, the goals of APT include establishing and spreading its bases within targeted firms' network or information technology infrastructure to harvest critical data. In the long run, APT attempts to harm, impede, or position itself to further manipulate the organization's IT network. As a result, an APT maintains its objectives by continually changing and maintaining the level of contact required to achieve them. Despite the different definitions, the common agreement is that APTs are deceptive cyber threats that break the security of computer networks using "low and sluggish" attacks that are difficult to detect until the breach is fully accomplished on the host network. This shows that APTs operate outside of the detection range of traditional IT security measures.

Advanced technology has yielded advanced computer networks. However, these networks are not immune from cyberattacks. The recent development in wireless communication technologies in intelligent transportation systems (ITS) has significantly influenced computer networks in the transport industry. Binevich and Vladyko (2019) highlighted the advanced communication technologies referred to as vehicular ad hoc networks (VANET) in motor transport. VANET/IT informs a driver of obstacles and helps in the determination of the safe course of action. Some of the cyberattack threats encountered by the VANET include Denial of Service (DoS), malware spamming, and illusion attack, among others. Disrupting the VANET/ITS network through DoS involves increasing delays in the network that make legitimate users' access to information impossible or difficult. Because information in vehicle wireless networks becomes obsolete so quickly, even minor delays might put a segment's activity to a halt because the road situation will have changed by the time the information is obtained. Binevich and Vladyko (2019) stated that the DoS attack lessens network availability and comes in various forms. Many researchers refer to all DoS attacks as routing or resource consumption. The DoS attack targets the wireless networks as they create massive information and demand from VANET/ITS the most resources to facilitate its processing.

The new generation networks often associated with mobile devices also encounter threats from cyberattacks and cyber-terrorism. Hraback et al. (2020) highlighted that new generation networks also referred to as 5G networks, are gradually becoming a part of our daily life. New 5G networks are hailed as a promising technology that combines many types of networks to give required functionality and applications. Intense transmission of IoT data transit will necessitate the deployment of alternative mobile networks such as Wireless Sensor Networks (WSN), Mobile Ad-Hoc Networks (MANET), and Drone Networks (DRONET) and exploiting their advantages. The consolidation of the various networks to form a multilayered network model would help reduce the undesired effects of cyberattacks, considering the essential services that could be dependent on these networks. Hraback et al. (2020) highlighted that the desire to provide uninterrupted services, especially during emergencies, could be made possible through a resilient multilayered network model. This model would ensure service provision even in the wake of unanticipated events. This model could be made up of Wireless Sensor Networks (WSN), and Mobile Ad-Hoc Networks (MANET). This model ensures reinforcement from cyberattacks and continued service delivery during the occurrence of such incidents.

Computer Systems

Computer systems are equally facing considerable threats from cyberterrorism and cyberattacks. A computer system refers to a collection of interconnected devices that process, store, and input data and information. These computer systems have been instrumental in the provision of crucial government functions, including critical infrastructures. As a result, compromised computer systems due to cyberattacks or cyberterrorism would disrupt essential services instrumental to human coexistence. Genge et al. (2012) highlighted the important role of Information and Communication Technologies (ICT) in operating modern Critical Infrastructures (CI), such as power plants, water plants, and smart grids because ICT can lead to cost savings as well as increased efficiency, flexibility, and interoperability. In the past, CIs existed in isolated environments and relied on protocols and reducing the threats to these systems. However, Networked Industrial Control Systems (NICS) are these days exposed to cyber threats that have been flagged by Supervisory Control and Data Acquisition (SCADA) systems. The disruption of the NICS is through several avenues, among them the Stuxnet worm. Genge et al. (2012) noted that the Stuxnet worm is the first malware formulated to cripple the NICS. Its ability to modify the logic of control hardware to change physical processes portrayed the potency of such threats. Stuxnet was a clear indication of a successful cyberattack. This malware requires a deep understanding of the physical system and software and operating system weaknesses. Power grids, transportation networks, and water supply systems rely on the computer control system to exert real-time monitoring and control. Reddy et al. (2021) highlighted that a Cyber-Physical System is formed by linking physical and cyber systems (CPS). Such coupling frequently introduces vulnerabilities, increasing the risk of physical system damage.

Computer systems thrive on interconnections, which attackers capitalize on. According to Reddy et al. (2021), several CIs are linked and reliant on one another. For instance, water treatment or water distribution system is dependent on power for operation and has a power connection to the distribution center. As a result, a random failure or cyberattack in a component of an interdependent system could have cascading effects, potentially causing a component or the entire system of interdependent CI to collapse. Determining the disruption effects of cyberattacks on critical infrastructures requires the examination of the interferences associated with cyberattacks on interconnected CIs. Reddy et al. (2021) highlighted physical dependence as one of the aspects that are adversely affected during a cyberattack. This aspect involves physical dependency on material flow from one CI to another, such as when an electric power grid provides electricity to water treatment and distribution systems. Cyber is the other interconnection of the critical infrastructure. According to Reddy et al. (2021), cyber, also referred to as informational dependency, refers to the dependency between two or more CI on each other for information flow. The authors noted that while interdependencies across CI are frequently required to achieve design standards, they can also result in unfavorable scenarios when a malfunction or attack in one CI spreads to other related CI. Due to the intricacy of the connected systems, such escalation may disrupt the operation of the relevant CI and create subtle feedback loops that might begin and propagate disturbances in unexpected ways. Reddy et al. (2021) noted that following the consolidation of cyber components like SCADA workstations, HMI interfaces, and PLCs, the critical infrastructure systems are more vulnerable to cyberattacks that could have undesirable effects.

The determination of dependencies highlighted in the critical infrastructures proves to be the starting point in unearthing the disruptions following cyberattacks and their impact on ordinary operations. This determination could involve security mechanisms in vehicle-to-grid infrastructure, vulnerability assessment in interdependent systems resilience assessment, and co-simulation for vulnerability analysis. Reddy et al. (2021) outlined the direct association between the assessment approaches and cybersecurity as the extracted dependencies could foster investigation of propaganda attacks throughout the systems. Mitigating the disruptions of cyberattacks on critical infrastructure has necessitated the development of frameworks capitalizing on open hybrid automata for modeling interdependency. Reddy et al. (2021) highlighted this model's utilization in examining the flowing effects through the interconnected CIs.

Modern computer systems such as the Internet of Things (IoT) increasingly encounter cyber threats in the form of cyberterrorism and cyberattacks. Although enabling communication between smart machines is a cutting-edge technology, the technologies that make up the Internet of Things are not new to us. As the name implies, IoT is a technique of translating data from several types of things to any virtual platform on today's internet infrastructure. Ahanger (2018) highlighted that the primary concept of IoT is to allow for the autonomous sharing of critical data between unseen embedded uniquely identifiable devices in the world while relying on prominent technologies such as Radio-Frequency Identification (RFID) and Wireless Sensor Networks (WSNs). The nature of the consolidation in the IoT increases vulnerabilities to cyberattacks. Ahanger (2018) noted that the sophistication associated with IoT emanates from the fact that combining various technologies into one is difficult, the system strives to securely link devices with limited computing, storage, and power. Few IoT devices have more than rudimentary security mechanisms, and some of them are incapable of maintaining the confidentiality and integrity of users' data. Privacy is a paramount concern gradually derailing the advancement of modern technologies. Most technologies in the past failed to ensure privacy and confidentiality, which resulted in significant impacts on the afflicted individuals. There are three fundamental aspects that elicit privacy and security concerns for IoT systems. Ahanger (2018) observed that in a threat from a malicious user, the owner of the IoT-device can launch attacks to obtain the device manufacturer's secrets and access to secret capabilities. The malicious user exposes the system's flaws in a bid to obtain information, sells knowledge to outside parties, and even attacks the system.

The second fundamental entity is the bad manufacturer. According to Ahanger (2018), the device creator can investigate the underlying technology to retrieve information from IoT devices or consumers. As previously stated, a manufacturer can purposefully create security flaws that can be exploited to gain access to the user's confidential information and even divulge it to third parties. Characteristically, the manufacture of poorly secured items compromises the privacy of their users. Furthermore, in the case of IoT, where different devices are linked to one another, a device manufacturer can target their competitors' gadgets simply to destroy their reputation. The third crucial entity is the external adversary, which is an external entity that is not a member of the system and does not have permission to use it. An adversary strives to obtain information about the users of the system. With vindictive intentions, such as causing financial losses and undermining the user's trustworthiness. The adversary causes weaknesses in the system by manipulating the sensed and communicated data. Ahanger (2018) cited that IoT devices could be crippled through device tampering. IoT devices are smaller devices infused in switches, cars, and TVs. With most IoT devices remaining unattended in most scenarios, they could be easily stolen without people noticing. If the device gets into the wrong hands, device tampering, software manipulation, and secret stealing could result in fake data being infused into a system. In business scenarios, cyberattacks targeting computer systems could have adverse impacts on an organizational system.

Citizens

Cyberattacks cripple and destroy the citizens in many ways that could be detrimental to their physical and emotional wellbeing. These attacks could result in the acquisition of confidential information for malicious or financial benefits. Cyberattacks could be targeting personal information from a person or group of people with a specific demographic profile for resale. Al-Eidi et al. (2020) noted that modern technology could result in the leakage of sensitive and confidential information. An individual's information that has been leaked to the public may find it difficult to continue with their lives as they did before. Their lives cease being private, and there are constantly scrutinized by the public due to their deeds that made them public. Reputations could be damaged, and people could lose the respect of their families, friends, and the entire community. A person who loses the respect of society and family may not see the need to continue leading a dissatisfactory life and could opt for the effortless way out, suicide. For others, they end up being depressed for their entire lives and cannot integrate with the society as they did before. The reputation damage is also devastating to employees of a given organization, especially when these companies seek to distance themselves from the leakage by laying off the affected employees. Vartolomei and Avasilcăi (2020) noted that a damaged organizational reputation due to a cyberattack might make it difficult for an entity to find customers to provide services to. The organization could be forced to close due to unproductivity, resulting in massive job losses.

Cyberattacks also elicit the possibility of identity theft. Identity theft refers to the situations where an imposter acquires sensitive and confidential information belonging to another person and creates another identity different from the actual owner of the stolen information. Identity theft could cripple a citizen's social and financial life, especially with details such as social security numbers, passwords, and account numbers getting into the wrong hands. Equifax (2021) stated that the severity of the repercussions of identity fraud would be determined by the type of crime committed. If fraudsters get direct access to your bank account or credit cards, one may find themselves without funds to cover basic living expenses. The article noted that identity theft has both short-term and long-term impacts. The stolen identity used in creating fake companies and getting into debt may affect an individual in the long run, especially when trying to start a business in an actual life scenario. An innocent victim could find themselves on the wrong side of the law, especially when their stolen identity is used to commit crimes. Equifax 920200 highlighted the case of an individual who spent a considerable time in incarceration trying to prove their innocence and distance themselves from crimes committed in their name. A stolen identity takes an emotional toll on a citizen. Victims of identity theft could struggle with anxiety issues, sleep disturbances, and elevated stress as they go through situations elicited by stolen identity. Myhre (2021) highlighted the skyrocketing incidences of social media identity theft. The article noted that more than 5% of consumers were victims of identity theft in 2019, resulting in about $17 million in losses. This figure was an increase of more than $2 million from the previous year. Citizens who have their identity stolen lead disoriented lives due to uncertainty of situations that could arise and compromise their employments, life situations, and interactions with others.

Identity theft disrupts a citizen's financial freedom due to its impact on credit history. According to Equifax (2021), identity theft can significantly impact one's credit score. If a fraudster utilizes existing credit or files for new credit with your information, your credit report may show debt or missed payments. Even if the criminal asks for credit and is denied, each application for credit is recorded, which can negatively impact credit history. Despite the possibility of correcting this information, speaking with the appropriate parties, and demonstrating that you have been a victim of crime can take time. Even a brief reduction in credit score, which lenders use to establish trustworthiness, might be problematic, especially if trying to open a new account, purchase a car, or apply for a mortgage. The recovery efforts translate to wasted opportunity, more disturbances, missed opportunities, sleeplessness, and running here and there when seeking assistance, all of which could be strenuous to a citizen.

A citizen's life is disrupted following ransomware attacks requiring them to pay up ransoms or risk their information being leaked to the public. Some citizens could be uncertain about the type of information the attackers could have and opt to pay ransoms to avoid the undesirable impacts. Considering the challenging economic circumstances some citizens go through, they may not have the required funds at their disposal. As such, they end up borrowing from families, friends, and financial institutions, which could affect them eventually. Due to dire situations, they could be encountering at the said time, victims of ransomware attacks may not pause to think about their ability to refund the borrowed money. As a result, citizens' credit scores could be affected, relationships with friends and families could be compromised, and the citizens could also develop mental health episodes due to the inability to pay borrowed funds. Healthcare data breaches significantly impact the health of patients and the wellbeing of their family members. HIPAA (2018) highlighted a study undertaken by Dr. Sung Choi, a researcher at Owen Graduate School of Management. Choi outlined data breaches as disorienting physicians, and the consequences of breaches can persist for years. According to Choi, HIPAA-covered organizations are facing investigations and litigation, which might cause medical services to be disrupted and treatment to be delayed. The cost of preventing attacks, such as purchasing new security solutions and dealing with the consequences of data breaches, can divert resources away from patient care. In the study, Choi analyzed hospital death rates before and after a data breach. The percentage of heart attack patients who died within 30 days of admission to the hospital was one of the criteria used to assess a potential drop in care quality. Choi added that the control group and breached hospitals had homogeneous mortality rates, yet following a data breach, the control group's mortality rate remained unchanged, while the mortality rate at breached hospitals increased. According to Choi's research, one year after a data breach, the death rate increased by 0.23 percent, and two years later, it increased by 0.36 percent. This translates to 2,160 deaths each year (HIPAA 2018).

The increased mortality could be attributed to numerous factors. First, the physicians could have delved more into unearthing intricate details about the data breach as opposed to providing the specialized care that the patients needed the most. Characteristically, the patients could have learned about the data breach and feared that their health was at risk, with increased worry and thoughts resulting in their health deterioration. In the study, Choi stated that following data breaches, the time taken to administer electrocardiographs for new patients was much longer (HIPAA 2018). An incident of a healthcare data breach could be compromising to patients who had opted to conceal the details of their health status to their family members to avoid worrying them. The incident could force them to speak out about their health to families who would opt to desert their employment and other life activities to be their full-time care providers. Being a care provider means that these family members may not lead their lives as they did before, and they may experience financial challenges as they do not have a source of income. They could also be in a constant state of worry due to getting the real glimpse of the actual health state of their loved one.

Service denial translates to frustrations while interfering with the citizens' livelihood. In the face of the ever-increasing number of Internet users and an ever-expanding range of Internet services, the demands on the security of users' data, services, and privacy are increasing as well. Fujdiak et al. (2021) highlighted Denial of Service (DoS) as one of the prominent cyberattacks. The primary intent of this attack is to make the targeted Internet service unavailable to other users, or at the very least, to reduce the service's quality and performance. DoS attacks are most directed at web servers to block people from accessing web content. Web, mail, database, file, and domain system servers and remote access services are the most common targets of DoS assaults. Internal network traffic on the target can also be blocked by attacks. In the modern world, DoS attacks could infect a considerable proportion of IoT (Internet of Things) devices. The processing resources and security levels on these devices are quite low. As a result, they are relatively easy to manage and manipulate for an assault. Despite their inability to create massive amounts of data traffic, these devices have more than enough capacity to launch a sluggish DoS attack.

As a result, IoT device security is a new challenge in the Cybersecurity area. The Distributed Denial of Service (DDoS) is another cyberattack targeting services most sought by the citizen, and which could give rise to disappointments and frustrations. Bonguet and Bellaiche (2017) noted that a DDoS is a DoS that employs many hosts to increase the impact of the attack. Hundreds of thousands of people can be found as hosts. Most of the time, the machine's owners are completely ignorant that their machines have been infected and compromised by a Trojan or a backdoor program. The acts that translate to a DDoS and aim at compromising the Cloud's availability can occur remotely or locally from a user's service. The victim's communication, computational resources, or network instructions are usually targeted.

The inability to obtain services can be overwhelming and frustrating, especially if there is an urgent need for the highlighted services. Some of the services sought from the websites could be detrimental to one's health, including booking healthcare appointments. The settling frustrations could be harmful to health and wellbeing as it could result in anxiety. While frustration is a common life experience, the ability to handle frustrations differs from one person to another. While one frustrated website user could be optimistic that services would be reinstated in time, another one would be disoriented, with panic attacks being the order of the day. A lot of time is also spent as one must reschedule some events to pave the way for actual visits to the hacked entities. Constant desire to continue pursuing the services despite the denial could translate to frustrations leading to other emotions such as aggressive behaviors. Business owners may not be able to recover from DoS attacks. The increased reliance on the internet has necessitated the automation of business processes, with most operations relying on websites to push their product and services globally. The reputational damage and increased costs of dealing with the impacts of DoS attacks could be overwhelming for a new entrepreneur. This citizen could opt to desert the organizational operations altogether and seek employment, which could be demoralizing and disappointing.

Leaked employee log-in credentials disrupt a citizen's life as the employee could be fired or incur fines for their recklessness. The leaked credentials could compromise the organizational operations, especially when sold to a competing company. Incidents of compromised credentials often occur due to employees being victims of phishing attacks or even their willingness to provide the same information at a fee. When credentials are lost, stolen, or disclosed, they might provide an intruder insider access. Although internal monitoring and analysis can discover unusual behavior, these credentials successfully bypass perimeter protection and make detection more difficult. A compromised credential's risk is proportional to the level of access it grants. Privileged access credentials, which grant administrative access to devices and systems, are usually more dangerous for businesses than consumer credentials. Humans are not the only ones who have login credentials. Passwords are frequently used to enable integration and communication between servers, network devices, and security solutions. These machine-to-machine credentials, when obtained by an attacker, can allow mobility throughout the company, both vertically and horizontally, granting unrestricted access.

The measures an organization takes to salvage the situation due to stolen log-in credentials could be detrimental to employees who have weak passwords or whose credentials have leaked. In avoiding such situations, organizations should sensitize the importance of strong passwords and avoid using common usernames such as nicknames and pet names. Organizations should ensure additional security measures that could include multiple authentications. Usernames should not be preserved on work desks or shared among different platforms the employees' access. Reduced network performance could potentially disrupt a citizen due to additional operational costs that could cripple a business after an extensive deficient performance. To meet the needs of its users, a business network must perform well.

Companies rely on network monitoring tools to observe their network's behavior and identify performance issues. However, it is imperative to determine other ways to boost a company's network performance. Arai (2022) outlined the strategy of balancing network maintenance costs and network performance loss in cutting on labor costs. Network performance can be improved in many ways, both significant and little. Depending on a company's requirements, one may wish to concentrate on various aspects of network performance. The network performance is detrimental to increased profits and overall customer satisfaction. Citizens who are frustrated due to poor network performance are bound to take businesses to entities with swift network performance, which could translate to a business loosening its loyal clientele base and having to close due to the inability to make satisfactory earnings. Optima network performance ensures seamless service provision. Affected employee productivity and customer experience due to poor network performance affect business operations. Such systems do not easily detect attacks, resulting in additional challenges, especially when not resolved in time. Arai (2022) suggested the adjustment of network layers to improve network performance and reduce impacts of poor network.

Dr. Tunde Alaofin

PROPOSED SOLUTIONS
AND PROTECTIONS

The CIA Triad

Solutions and protections aimed at safeguarding against cyberterrorism and cyberattacks should consider the involved entities and its resource capabilities, infrastructure, and available security policies. However, there are general cybersecurity models that could apply to the government, corporations, and individuals. One of such is the CIA Triad model. The term is in no way associated with the United States intelligence agency. Instead, the CIA stands for confidentiality, integrity, and availability. These three concepts, when taken together, form the foundation of any organization's security architecture.

Moreover, CIA Triad should serve as goals and objectives for every security program. The CIA triad is so fundamental to information security that one can be certain that one or more of these principles has been undermined whenever data is leaked, a system is attacked, a user falls for phishing bait, an account is hijacked, any other security incidents occur. The CIA triad is a well-known information security paradigm that can help an organization's actions and policies to keep its data safe. The CIA Triad is also a data security benchmark model that governs and evaluates how an organization handles data as it is stored, transmitted, or processed. Each of the triad's attributes indicates a crucial aspect of information security. Andress (HHH) highlighted that the CIA triad provides a model for facilitating discussions and thoughts on security concepts. This model provides a discussion of security concepts through the aspects of confidentiality, integrity, and availability.

I. Confidentiality

These aspects relate to ensuring that only the authorized individual shave access to data and computer systems. Bragg 9HHH0 observed that confidentiality simply means that the exchanged data is solely read and sent to authorized individuals. In practice, confidentiality means restricting data access to prevent illegal disclosure. Confidentiality entails ensuring that only authorized individuals have access to specified assets and that unauthorized individuals are actively prevented from gaining access. Andress 9HHH) highlighted the similarity between privacy and confidentiality concept. The confidentiality implementation differs at various levels of the process. The text highlighted the different confidentiality levels involved in the undertaking of a bank ATM withdrawal transaction. A bank customer ensures confidentiality during withdrawal through a personal identification number (PIN). The PIN alongside the ATM card enables the cash withdrawal. Characteristically, the ATM owner ensures confidentiality with regards to the account balance and any other information crucial to the communication with the bank from which the withdrawal is made. The bank maintains the confidentiality of the transaction with the ATM (Andresshhh). In case the transaction's confidentiality is compromised, the aftermath would be unfavorable to the individual, ATM owner, and the bank.

A key aspect of ensuring confidentiality is making sure that those who do not have the necessary authorization cannot access assets that are crucial to a company. On the other hand, an effective system guarantees that those who require access have the required permissions. Confidentiality protection relies on the ability to define and enforce access levels for information for confidentiality protection. In certain circumstances, this entails sorting information into different collections according to who needs access to it and the data's sensitivity. That is, the degree of damage that would be caused if the confidentiality were to be compromised. Gladden (2017) highlighted that the CIA triad became prominent in the 1970s as practical assistance for ensuring the security of electronic computers involved in processing critical and sensitive data. Confidentiality could be compromised in several ways, including direct attacks aimed at gaining access to a system the hacker has no permission to access. Andress (2011) observed that confidentiality could also be compromised due to the loss of a laptop or any other device providing access to a computer system. Additional circumstances include people peeping as another person is typing their password, sending an e-mail attachment to the wrong person and an attackers' penetration into the systems. Bragg added that confidentiality could also be compromised through the intentional disclosure of information or lax security procedures. The author techniques such as network security protocols, network authentication services, and encryption services as measures of safeguarding confidentiality.

II. Integrity

Data integrity represents 'I' in the CIA triad. Integrity is an essential aspect of the CIA Triad because it protects data from unauthorized deletion or modification, and it assures that if an authorized individual initiates a change that should not have been made, the damage can be undone. Integrity also involves the maintenance of data in a correct state, and no one should be able to alter it inappropriately, either mistakenly or maliciously. Characteristically, integrity also involves upholding the data's trustworthiness by ensuring it is reliable and untampered with. The data integrity is upheld if it is original, accurate, and dependable data maintains the integrity of your data. The information provided on an organization's website needs to have integrity to ensure that customers, employees, and industry stakeholders perceive an organization as untrustworthy. The website also provides an avenue for interfering with an organization's integrity. Cybercriminals could hack an organization's website and alter information to compromise the reputation of the organization. Employees and/or shareholders, eliciting concerns of untrustworthy. Andresss (2011) noted that integrity protection necessitates the development of measures to curb unauthorized data changes but also has in place mechanisms to reverse data changes that need to be undone. Bragg (2003) suggested firewall systems, communication systems, and intrusion detection frameworks as some of the techniques to uphold data integrity. Andresss (2011) noted that data integrity is overly important, especially when it is the foundation of an organization's crucial decision-making. Compromising integrity is often intentional. To conceal intrusion, an attacker could circumvent an intrusion detection system (IDS), change file configurations to allow unauthorized access or manipulate the system's logs. Integrity can also be harmed by chance. Someone may inadvertently enter the incorrect code or make another careless error. In addition, if the company's security policies, controls, and procedures are insufficient, integrity might be compromised without anyone in the organization being held responsible.

III. Availability

Availability refers to data being accessible to authorized users whenever they need it. When a legitimate request is made, data should be made available. It ensures that when data is needed, authorized parties have unrestricted access. Destruction attacks target availability. Confidentiality and integrity are crucial, with availability making the CIA triad complete. Even if data is secured and its integrity is preserved, it is often meaningless unless it is accessible to those within the business as well as the served clients. As a result, systems, networks, and applications must all work properly and at the appropriate times. Individuals who have access to specific data must also be able to consume it when they need it and accessing the data should not take an excessive amount of time. Andress (2011) observed that the availability loss could involve the various breaks in any chain that enables the data access. Such situations could emanate from power loss, operating systems, application difficulties, and a compromised system. The author highlighted the attacks from an outside attacker compromising the data availability as referred to as Denial of Service (DoS) attacks. Bragg (2003) observed that despite availability not being considered a security professional area due to the prevalence of DoS attacks, the need for continuous data presence is crucial. Some techniques for ensuring data availability could include reliability and functionality in security processes and mechanisms and fault tolerance in disks, systems, and backup.

THEORIES ON INFORMATION SECURITY POLICIES AND GUIDELINES

Modern society is significantly reliant on computers and global networks. As a result, the information required in this society. As a result, information systems are required to ensure the shared information's confidentiality, integrity, and availability. Violation of information security could result in the compromised safety of the organization's information and an individual whose information has been compromised. Leaked personal information could damage the organization's reputation, interfering with its business operations and the ability to make profits. It is paramount to ensure the security of an organization's information system. The organization should implement several safety security system policies. However, these efforts could be rendered futile, especially if the organization lacks security policies to ensure strict adherence to security policies. An information security policy (ISP) establishes rules and procedures for employees, establishing a standard for appropriate use of the company's information technology, such as networks and apps, to preserve data confidentiality, integrity, and availability. This policy also ensures a unified effort towards safeguarding an organization's information. The constant threat evolution necessitates compliance requirements that are becoming more complicated. In dealing with concerns of compliance and threats, large and small businesses must develop a comprehensive security program. It is impossible to organize and enforce a security program across a business without an information security policy. It is also impossible to convey security measures to third parties and external auditors without such a program in place. Peltier (2004) highlighted the information protection program as the larger umbrella incorporating information policies classified depending on an individual's position in an organization. According to the author, this program is not developed to fulfill security needs or auditing requirements. Instead, it is a business program equipping the organization with the processes required to undertake its function while maintaining its position as a trusted entity.

An information security policy oversees data protection, one of the numerous assets that a company must safeguard. An organization that attempts to create a working information security policy must have well-defined security and strategic objectives. Management must agree on these goals, as any existing differences in this area could jeopardize the project's success. The most important thing for a security expert to keep in mind is that understanding security management techniques would foster their inclusion into the documents one is tasked with drafting. This ensures completeness, quality, and applicability. The policy should ideally be written in a concise and to-the-point manner. Documents with redundant text can become extensive and illegible, and having too many additional details can make full compliance difficult. The management's perception of IT security is one of the essential things to consider in implementing IT security standards. Security experts need to ensure that the information security policy is treated with the same importance as other corporate rules. When an organization has a large structure, policies may differ and must be separated to define dealings within the desired subset of the company. Bayuk and ProQuest (2012) highlighted the different applications of the term security in various aspects relating to cybersecurity. Policies could also be the laws and regulations and objectives on information protection. The information security policies align with the CIA triad as they strive to protect the information's confidentiality, integrity, and availability.

Information security policy is an area impacting every individual with direct and indirect interaction with an organization. Conscious and unconscious acts of these individuals potentially impact an organization's information security. Security awareness is a crucial aspect involving the organizational stakeholders and their various levels of interactions with an organization. Communicating IT security policy is a remarkable effort in an organization. Making employees read and acknowledge a paper on security policies does not indicate familiarity and comprehension of security policies. On the other hand, a training session would engage staff and ensure that they are aware of the protocols and methods in place to protect data. An awareness training session should include a wide range of critical issues, such as gathering, using, and destroying data, data quality, records management, confidentiality, privacy, acceptable use of IT systems, and proper social networking usage. It could be a clever idea to include a brief test at the conclusion. Awareness training on information security could improve the decision-making aspect. According to Tsohou and Holtkamp (2018), information system users make frequent decisions on compliance and non-compliance of information system protections to protect information system (IS) resources. Several theories exist to explain the various interactions with information systems.

Bulgurcu *et al.* (2010), as cited by Tsohou and Holtkamp (2018), detailed the neoclassical economics rational choice theory in relation to IS. The theory denoted the utilization of rational decision-making on complying or not complying with security policies, depending on the perceived benefits and costs attributed to compliance or non-compliance. The article added that the conscious decisions on compliance or non-compliance of information security policies depend on benefits, barriers, and individual capacities. Agboola (2015) observed that the rational economic man in neoclassic economics capitalizes on self-interest as a means of maximizing utility. In achieving the said utility, the rational man does not align with groups of individuals. The author noted that despite people not always acting in pursuit of self-interest, people tend to make choices depending on self-interests and other remote and moral reasons not associated with personal gains. As a result, in striving to ensure adherence to information security policies (ISPs), it is paramount to consider personal interests and the school of thought an individual subscribes to.

Protection motivation theory also aligns with the different reasons motivating adherence to ISPs. Tsohou and Holtkamp (2018) stated that this theory denotes people as undertaking individual threat assessments to determine the necessity of embracing measures to protect the information assets through compliance to the security policy. During these assessments, the employees and other involved individuals evaluate the threat-related aspects and the countermeasures enforced by the ISP. The article highlighted the suggestion by the ISP literature that people do not blindly comply with ISPs and undertake personal assessments and decisions before undertaking a security behavior related to a security policy. Zhang et al. (2020) highlighted the prominence of the protection motivation theory (PMT) in denoting an individual's behavior and intention in portraying protective behavior. Concerning PMT, an individuals' assessments of the severity of prospective dangers following a threat appraisal and their ability to exhibit specific coping behaviors in the face of threats after a coping appraisal determine their willingness to engage in protective activity. Lee (2011), as cited by Zhang et al. (2020), noted that perceived vulnerability and perceived severity are often included in threat assessments. Perceived vulnerability refers to an individuals' perceptions of their exposure to a negative danger. On the other hand, perceived severity is the magnitude of the repercussions of a threat. Characteristically, coping appraisal often includes three basic elements: response cost, response efficacy, and self-efficacy. Good and Hyman (2020) added that the prevailing assumption in PMT is that people will protect themselves from a sufficient level of physical, psychological, or social threat. According to the theory, fear appeals activate cognitive assessment procedures that consider the threat's potency, the likelihood of occurrence, and vulnerability in responses recommendation. Protection motivation (people's intentions to protect against dangers signaled by fear appeals) is induced by threat and coping appraisals, encouraging desirable behaviors. The behaviors include means of coping with threats and reduce their effects rather than denials or avoidance behaviors meant to manage unpleasant emotions.

Competence is a crucial factor to consider in determining adherence to information security policy (ISP). Compliance is dependent on an individual's skills and capabilities. The competence influences the threat assessment to determine the best course of action. Tsohou and Holtkamp (2018) observed that gauging individuals' competencies in security improvement coincide with the recent guidance on information security governance frameworks. The ISO 27001 (2013) necessitates an organization to determine the competencies of every organization, and which could influence their information security performance. Rational choice theory (RCT) is one of the many theories relating to the human aspect of information system protection (ISP) in organizations. Individuals rely on their logic and judgment, which is informed by cost-benefit evaluations. Hyungjin and Han (2019) highlighted the ISP application of the rational choice theory in explaining the three primary factors influencing the employees' compliance with ISP behaviors.

These factors include the perceived compliance cost, perceived benefits of compliance, and the perceived costs attributed to non-compliance. The authors noted that additional factors might play a role in the relationship between perceived compliance costs and ISP compliance intentions, although little research has been done on this topic. Kristic and Kristic (2015) observed that individual rational behavior is linked to the methodological individualism premise, which states that all social phenomena may be explained in terms of individual activity. From the highlighted school of thought, the rational choice theory perceives the world as a strategic arena for maximizing individual interests. Social behavior is mostly logical, with emotion playing a residual influence, and actors intentionally strive to maximize their usefulness in a resource-constrained context. Their preferences determine the actors' aims. The amount of gathered information determines the chosen alternative. The players in the rational choice model are supposed to have the optimal quantity of information. On the other hand, real individuals do not have all the required information or are inaccurate and unreliable. Hyungjin and Han (2019) outlined that the rational choice theory was developed by Becker (1968) with the central notion that lawbreakers examine costs and benefits attributed to deviant behaviors before settling on whether to offend. It, therefore, means that people make reasonable judgments about the effects of their actions based on cost-benefit evaluations and act accordingly. Individuals weigh the costs of ISP noncompliance, such as sanctions or data exposure to security concerns, against the benefits, such as convenience or cost and time savings, when it comes to non-compliant ISP activity.

The general deterrence theory (GDT) is an additional theory used in the exploration of ISP antecedents. Hyungjin and Han (2019) highlighted that the prevailing assumption in the GDT theory is on the fundamental rationality of human beings and their tendency to unearth deterrent certainty and severity to examine the right course of action following the occurrence of a rule violation. Punishment, as a deterrent aspect, acts as a precursor to desired actions in GDT. On the other hand, the outcomes of GDT-based research are mixed. Herath and Rao (2009), as cited by Hyungjin and Han (2019), observed that GDT factors, including punishment severity and detection, often influence compliance to ISP. In information security, employing the GDT is instrumental in understanding the organizational insiders' behaviors. Burns et al. (2017) observed that organizations capitalizing on a GDT framework in their security efforts perceive their employees as an information system risk and aim to mitigate these risks by employing sanctions. A deterrent-based security approach aims to assure security by imposing punishments on any employee who engages in specific forbidden activities. These activities could include unauthorized access and internally abusing computer systems. Yu (1994), as cited by Burns et al. (2017), outlined that the deterrence theory focuses on three dimensions: speed, certainty, and severity.

Consequently, it implies that swift, certain, and punitive punishment discourages individuals penalized individuals from violating again (specific deterrence) and deters the broader public from committing crimes (generic deterrence). Sikolia et al. (2018) observed that the deterrence theory capitalizes on the thought that people consider the costs and rewards before engaging in criminal activity and select crime if it pays. As a result, if a person believes there is a high chance of being caught and the punishment is harsh, they will refrain from engaging in unlawful activities. More severity and certainty of punishment after committing a crime would make people refrain from committing a crime.

The protection motivation theory (PMT), general deterrence theory (GDT), and rational choice theory (RCT) all narrow down to behavior change as the focal point of successful information security policies (ISPs). Organizations should consider these theories in initiating ISPs efforts in an organization. Sommestad et al. (2014) highlighted the importance of having specifics when implementing an organizational ISP. The policy should cover topics such as the ramifications of security policy violations, permissible use of computer resources, information security obligations, and the training that employees of various categories should get. The core premise is that adhering to an acceptable information security policy will improve the organization's information security. On the other hand, organizational compliance with information security policies is far from simple. Implementation of information system police to enforce cybersecurity requires the cooperation of the organizational stakeholders and the different capacities in an organization. Policies serve as the foundation for programs, offering direction, consistency, and clarity in an organization's operations. They provide your staff with consistent methods for controlling legal and compliance risk as a set of internal standards. Knowing what an information security policy is and what it should include will enable employees and all organizational stakeholders to protect sensitive information more effectively as compliance matures.

Individuals in different capacities in an organization have an instrumental and distinctive role in ensuring the effective implementation of the information protection policies (IPSs). As a result, assisted at the organizational level should be dependent on the holding capacity. According to Sommestad et al. (2014), organizational decision-makers require instruction on best achieving compliance with their information security policy and deter misuse. The bone of contention in implementing IPSs is ensuring the contribution of employees, leadership, and the availability of resources to take through the implementation process. Rao et al. (2020) highlighted information security behaviors as made up of psychological components. Therefore, the protections and solutions for governments, corporations, and individuals should consider psychological behaviors and the unique attributes of the involved entity.

PROTECTIONS AND SOLUTIONS APPLICABLE TO THE GOVERNMENT

The government has been on the receiving end in relation to the fair share of cyberterrorism and cyberattack incidents. Safeguarding against cyberattacks could require a multi-faceted approach that could necessitate implementing a cyber-security strategy, collaborating with other countries, investing in infrastructure developments, and undertaking a comprehensive training awareness. A successful cybersecurity strategy for the government would necessitate corporation between the citizens and government officials. Characteristically, launching a countrywide campaign on cybersecurity would help sensitize some of the minor ignored aspects that could potentially compromise the country's cybersecurity and adversely affect critical infrastructures. Lots of vetting may be required to ensure that hired government officials are those with the capacity and desire to ensure total protection of the government operations. However, all these efforts would be fruitless without the key crucial cybersecurity aspects requiring the government's consideration. The employed measure should be distinguished for the national and local government. While some mechanisms could be effective for the local government, they could not provide adequate protection for the national government and the hefty critical infrastructures under its operations.

I.   The government should have a proactive approach to cybersecurity threats. Major incidents can be avoided by taking a proactive security posture. Implemented preventative measures foresee probable situations and safeguard from terrible catastrophes that could result in disruption of services, identity theft, and compromised computer systems. The deterrents of a proactive security system could include having agencies that flag off cyber-security threats before causing damage. The proactive approach could also include the active monitoring of threats to determine patterns and trends that could derail similar attacks in the future. The monitoring should be conducted 24 hours a day, seven days a week, and all the days of the month. An example is the NSA's Cybersecurity Threat Operations Center (NCTOC). Cybersecurity Operations (n.d.) observed that NCTOC develops and implements strategic security measures for the nation's most robust networks by leveraging unique insights into adversary intents and tradecraft. NCTOC provides fully equipped teams who work with US Cyber Command to protect the unclassified Department of Defense Information Network (DoDIN), a global network with 3 million users in locations ranging from offices in Washington, DC, to war zones in Afghanistan. The protection by this agency focuses on the functions under this agency.

II.   Ensuring a culture of cybersecurity vigilance among government officials. Achieving cybersecurity vigilance would involve ensuring government staff receive training on cybersecurity standards and collaborate with experts to establish effective cyber-resilience procedures. Multi-factor authentication, for example, can be extremely advantageous. Just like any other cultural change, cybersecurity vigilance would require the commitment and involvement of the leadership in government officials. Mehan (2014) observed that if cybersecurity is not prioritized at the executive level, it is unlikely to be successful. The cybersecurity culture would require setting the right tone by the leadership. Poor leadership could derail the much-needed culture change despite how much a cybersecurity culture could be needed and how good the cybersecurity principles could be. Mehan (2014) highlighted that a cybersecurity strategy could only be successful if using a holistic top-up and bottom-down formulated by the management and can only thrive through an environment of positive leadership and proactive information governance. All the government staff should be involved in protecting crucial government information. According to Batteau (2011), security culture is partially the mindset and social connection. While it would be the individual responsibility of the stakeholders to initiate efforts such as updating the antivirus software, it all narrows down to the availability of the resources. The management's commitment would ensure the availability of resources when and if needed.

III.   Encrypting sensitive information. Government operations require exchanging information from one agency to another, increasing data's vulnerability while on transit. In protecting the data during such movements, the government should consider data encryption. Data encryption eliminates the possibility of the leakage of sensitive information that could compromise operations due to the crippling of critical infrastructures associated with the leaked information. Encryption is a cybersecurity measure that protects private and personal data by scrambling it with unique codes that make it impossible for unauthorized individuals to read. Even if a data breach occurs, encryption ensures that an institution's private data remains secure, even if attackers manage to breach the firewall. Management Association & Information Resources (2021) observed that encryption ensures data protection in transit or storage. The data encryption procedure is simple. The plaintext data is translated into unreadable data using an encryption key and a specific encryption technique. Intruders will not be able to read the data if they get past the system security measures because the jumbled data can only be decoded using the associated encryption key. Maleh et al. (2021) noted that internal cybersecurity measures in a Big Data Environment, such as encryption of sensitive information using Hardware Secure Module (HSM), involves using keys for encrypting content, whether transactions or data preserved in a disk, application, or storage key. Wang et al. (2019) stated that data encryption on the Internet of Things (IoT) primarily entails encrypting information and authenticating messages to provide information security and detect data tampering.

IV. Encouraging the use of a strong password. Using passwords is not an adequate measure of protecting government systems, data, and computer networks. The passwords should be strong enough to safeguard them from unauthorized intrusion. Characteristically, the handling of these passwords should be in a manner aimed at ensuring cybersecurity. Passwords should not be pet names, dates of birth, or even favorite colors. This information is something an attacker could easily guess and becomes the first trial attempt when trying to log into a computer. Passwords are a computer's and personal information's first line of defense against unwanted access. A computer will be safer from hackers and malware if protected by a strong password. All accounts on a computer should use strong passwords. Common hackers will find it difficult to break into a machine if the password is tough to guess, forcing them to find another target. The more complex the password, the less likely it is that an unwanted infiltration will occur on one's computer. However, Ayyagari et al. (2019) observed that people ignore the best information practices by creating weak passwords. Despite the importance of strong passwords, the detailed author research denoted the tendency to use, share, and reuse weak passwords. Despite the convenient and effortless way of using passwords as a form of authentication, people are bad at passwords management. In adhering to the requirement of creating strong passwords, people may create complex passwords that could be difficult to remember. Fagan et al. (2017) highlighted the recommendation of using password managers to deal with the challenge of remembering many and unique passwords.

V.   Using two-factor authentication. In recent years, there has been a significant surge in cyberattack incidences culminating in personal information loss. Companies are discovering that their outdated security solutions are no match for contemporary threats and attacks as cybercrime becomes more sophisticated. It is not uncommon for them to be revealed due to simple human error. User trust is not the only thing that can be harmed. Global corporations, small enterprises, and government agencies can all incur significant financial and reputational damage. Two-factor authentication is an additional layer of protection that verifies that anyone attempting to access an online account are who they claim to be. The user must first provide their username and password. They will then be requested to submit another piece of information before they can receive access. Sidi et al. (2020) added that 2-FA ensures users provide two pieces of information or credentials during the login process as a security measure. Waleed (2019) observed that despite username and password being the common authentication method, they are vulnerable to eavesdropping and replay attacks. The 2FA could also send a computer-generated code to a user's phone or email address and be prompted to input the code into the website for a successful login. These instructions aim at achieving an alignment between the login credentials and provided code. The second factor could also be in the form of security questions about the user or something they know. A login is unsuccessful due to a compromise of any of the two factors.

VI. Intergovernmental organization cooperation. Cybersecurity in government should be enhanced through the cooperation between national and local governments and government agencies. This cooperation ensures the consolidation of resources and expertise in the fight against cyberterrorism and cyberattacks. The collaboration also ensures a united front, making it easy to win the war. Cybercrime poses a significant threat to the global economy. Individuals, businesses, key infrastructure, and governments are all affected. In addition to causing direct harm, cybercrime is a significant obstacle to digital trust, weakening the benefits of online, increasing inequality, and impeding international attempts to maintain cyber stability. To effectively combat this threat, it is critical to enhance cybercrime's cost and the risks that cybercriminals face. This can only be accomplished through successful public-private partnerships, with businesses collaborating with law enforcement. This program intends to accelerate the formation of a public-private partnership to tackle cybercrime. Prominent law enforcement agencies, international organizations, cybersecurity enterprises, service and platform providers, global entities could be part of the partnership. The time needed to develop trust between the government and private cooperation may be long, and the cybersecurity reinforcement does not enjoy the luxury of time. In starting, the partnerships could be between government agencies. DHS (2011) highlighted the cooperation between state and federal organizations in protecting government networks. In

December 2009, the DHS launched a first federal-state cybersecurity partnership to dispatch the DHS's EINSTEIN 1 cybersecurity system to Michigan's government networks. DHS's U.S. Computer Emergency Readiness Team (US-CERT) will flag off possible unusual activities on Michigan's networks and deal with threats to critical cyber infrastructure as part of the partnership with Michigan, to reinforce defenses against cyberattacks and the resilience of networks and cyber resources in Michigan.

VII. Promotion of public awareness on cybersecurity: Most incidences of compromised cybersecurity emanate from a lack of adequate knowledge on the required measures to enhance cybersecurity. The sensitization should be followed up with continued training to ensure the involved parties are reminded of cybersecurity measures. Cybersecurity awareness entails empowering people associated with an entity to play a part in defense against potential security threats. Credential formulation, resources, training, and technologies are used to give insights and actions on defense provision through Cybersecurity awareness. Communication is a significant component of information security awareness. Every government staff should be aware of the government's common values, including the right to privacy, and their role in preserving these values. A successful security awareness campaign promotes the government's principles through interactive platforms such as face-to-face dialogues and online communications. CISA (2021) highlighted October as a cybersecurity awareness month known as the National Cybersecurity Awareness Month in the past. During this month, there are continued efforts to increase awareness about the importance of cybersecurity throughout the United States, ensuring that all Americans have access to the tools they need to be safe and secure

111

online. DHS (2011) highlighted The Department of Homeland Security's commitment to finding new and inventive ways to raise public awareness about the need to protect America's computer systems and cyber networks against cyberattacks.

VIII. Cybersecurity workforce development (CWD): CWD focuses on establishing the finest methodologies and technologies to assist organizations in cultivating the knowledge and skills their cyber workforce requires to handle today's increasing cyber problems. Cyber technology is progressing at a faster rate than it has in the past. The proliferation of software in individuals' daily lives and the expansion of software systems have increased the number of flaws and vulnerabilities that cyber attackers can misuse. These attackers, varying from cybercriminals to state actors, are constantly developing new ways to compromise networks. DHS (2011) highlighted that this department narrows down to sourcing a broad collection of cybersecurity professionals, including computer engineers, analysts, and scientists. These professions help secure the nation's digital assets and protect against cyber threats facing critical infrastructure and important resources.

IX. Updated security solutions: Governments should finance cybersecurity solutions to protect sensitive data instead of relying on outdated and potentially susceptible security practices. Shrobe et al. (2017) highlighted the development of strict data security measures and adhering to data security measures as the essential aspects of success in the future. The text highlighted the importance of new tools and technologies to conduct transparent analysis. The innovative solutions would help audit and track information and facilities management and data sharing in the future. Outdated software is more vulnerable to cyberattacks such as malware and ransomware. The obsolete software provides a backdoor for resetting the software.

Dr. Tunde Alaofin

PROTECTIONS AND SOLUTIONS APPLICABLE TO THE CORPORATIONS

Organizations have increasingly encountered serious cyberattacks in recent years or increasing the possibility of an attack due to weak cyber-security policies. Despite growing knowledge of the repercussions of cyberattacks, it is becoming increasingly of a problem. Organizations are putting additional efforts to reinforce their cybersecurity efforts as a means of safeguarding from cyberattacks. Cyberattacks are not specific. As denoted by recent data breaches, organizations of all types, sizes, and locations are vulnerable to cyberattacks at any time. The vulnerability in all companies is due to the general reluctance of employees to embrace formulated cybersecurity measures such as strong passwords. Some corporations are so fixated on acquiring sophisticated equipment and cybersecurity software and disregard the basic practices compromising the organization's cybersecurity. The following are the practical solutions and protection measures an organization could embrace.

I.   Creating a cybersecurity awareness program. This program should apply to both the organizational employees and leadership. IT solutions can go as far as seamless implementation and acceptance by the employees and the leadership. Most of the most basic cyberattacks may be avoided through adherence to existing policies and procedures and the increased recognition of the crucial role played by an organization's people in an effective cyber-security plan. However, reinforcing regulations and limits is not the only way to reduce the risks or vulnerabilities caused by your employees, which could be detrimental to the organization's overall cybersecurity. Instead, creating an effective security culture requires increasing cyber risk awareness and comprehension and integrating security knowledge on attitudes and behaviors throughout an organization. Vasileiou and Furnell (2019) highlighted the lack of cybersecurity awareness and adherence to the same as the primary cause of breaches and cyberattack incidents. The authors noted that despite recognizing the problem, the measures developed in mitigating this challenge do not follow the expected steps and embrace the desired level of seriousness. The authors highlighted the common utilization of the SETA acronym (security, education, training, and awareness) as an inclusive factor in the measures in resolving the cyberattack incident. Most organizations do not accord cybersecurity awareness the level of importance it deserves. When employees do something as basic as clicking a link in an email message that seems to come from an internal organizational member or an outside entity, they unknowingly become contributors to a malware assault.

The methods used by cybercriminals to intrude networks are growing more sophisticated. The human resources department, procurement, and other departments could be potential targets due to their minimal understanding of the hazards faced due to breaches. Organizations must communicate and perform frequent and progressive educational sessions to equip employees with the various strategies used by cybercriminals and instill a culture of risk awareness in their workforce. According to Vasileiou and Furnell (2019), the impacts of an unaware and non-compliant employee concerning cybersecurity measures are significant as they compromise others and potentially endanger organizational operations. The development of cybersecurity awareness should stem from the provision of training and education by capitalizing on the acceptable guidelines on technology utilization and password security practices. Depending on the intricate data an organization handles, cybersecurity measures could be tailored to an organization's unique needs and operations.

II. Sensitizing on strong but easy-to-remember passwords. Employees often go for simple passwords that could be easy to remember. However, these passwords end up being weak and shared in various lengths in requirements, increasing vulnerabilities for cyberattacks. An attacker with adequate knowledge of an employee could easily get into their computer systems by inputting birth data, favorite color, or pet's name. Good and strong passwords help eliminate unauthorized access. However, creating and remembering secure passwords for all online accounts could be a real challenge. The basic steps in preparation for a cyberattack could involve protecting all devices with a complex password, which is only shared with the device user. The password should be memorized as opposed to writing it down somewhere easily accessible. Employees should not underestimate the power of physically connecting computers to desks. Weisbaum (2019) observed that according to an online specialist on password protection, people prefer simple and easy, something that does not augur well with passwords. Most people consider passwords to be a problematic aspect of utilizing technology, although they serve a purpose. However, they are frequently misapplied in daily business activities. Many businesses make the error of giving all employees default and easily guessed passwords and fail to encourage or push them to update them regularly. Organizations should place more emphasis on setting strong, unique passwords for all business-related software and devices. Also, measures should be implemented to ensure the regular alteration of the passwords through manual or automated mechanisms. Strong passwords should be at least ten characters long and include a combination of upper- and lower-case letters, numbers, and other symbols. Weisbaum (2019) discourage reusing passwords is prone to phishing attacks or data breach.

III. Frequent monitoring of backups and security systems. One thing that could be most disappointing to the organization is to imagine that the backup and security system is in place, only to be disappointed in its disorientation when needed. Organizations may not detect cybersecurity attacks for the unmonitored backup security systems, including data tampering and initiating the right corrective measures. Characteristically, it would be so disappointed when there is nothing to salvage after a cyberattack and data loss leaves the organization in much need of backup systems. Regular testing of backup and security systems should be incorporated as part of an organizational IT policy framework to eliminate the vulnerabilities and weaknesses of the backup and security systems, increasing susceptibility to cyberattacks. Data should be safeguarded against unintentional data loss, corruption, and unauthorized access. These efforts could include the regular production of extra copies of data to restore the original data or recover earlier versions of the data. A backup is a copy of the data on a system or network that can restore a file or archive the same. Backups are a critical component of a business continuity plan since they enable for protection and recovery of data.

The ongoing possibility of data alteration or erasure due to persistent and intentional deletions, malware, ransomware, natural disasters, or other occurrences necessitates backups. An organization should develop several methods and tools to back up sensitive data and recover it on time. Backups protect an organization's data from loss or alteration, provide an effective way to recover deleted or corrupted files. Idemudia (2019) emphasized the importance of ensuring regular backups to safeguard against the undesired impacts of cyberattacks. The author suggested the peer-to-peer (P2P) due to its reliability and security as a backup system due to the reliance on the hard disk space connected to the internet to implement distributed backup services. Idemudia (2019) observed that the backup system processes' consistency should depend on the availability requirements while routinely testing the restoration procedures to maintain the backup's integrity. The cybersecurity strategy should also incorporate the discarding of backed-up data. According to Idemudia (2019), discarded computer disks face a possibility of compromising the stored sensitive information. Kljun, Mariani, and DDix (2016), as cited by III, noted that a fifth of the computers in the study was not backed up, and it could be impossible to restore a quarter of the important files following their accidental or intentional deletion.

IV. Using updated and original software. To save the extra coin, the organization could tend to use old and cheap software that has several loopholes and increase susceptibility to cyberattacks. Organizational employees are not new to the routine pop-ups reminding of software updates. While undertaking other tasks, the employees could be tempted to click the 'remind me later' option, which is a cybersecurity threat every time there is a delay in a software update. The continued procrastination eliminates the possibility that the software update is ever done. The importance of software upgrades to an organization's digital safety and Cybersecurity cannot be overstated. The sooner the update, the more secure the device, computer systems, and network could be— at least until the next update notice. Lee (2013) highlighted the importance of ensuring up-to-date software by allowing automatic updates and accepting updates anytime a reminder popup from the service provider, manufacturer, and the application provider. Despite the additional time required during the software update process, many benefits are accrued from the same. Updates to software provide numerous advantages. It's all about the rewrites. Repairing security gaps that have been identified and correcting or deleting computer bugs are examples of these tasks. Updates can introduce recent features to one's device while also removing old ones. It is also imperative to ensure an organization's operating system is up to date while undertaking updates.

Hackers thrive on identified security flaws on a computer system or data storage. A software vulnerability is a flaw or security opening identified in a program or operating system. Hackers can exploit the flaw by developing a code to exploit the vulnerability. Malware is often used in the packaging of the code. With the security flaws due to updated software, a simple act of redirecting to a rogue website, opening a corrupted message, or playing media is enough to open the computer system to hacking and data theft attempts. Selfish employees look at the additional time they would spend updating software and forget that it is not solely about them. The stolen data could compromise additional individuals and damage the organization's reputation.

V.   Awareness of cybersecurity strengths and weaknesses. An organization's knowing its capabilities and shortcomings concerning cybersecurity is a step towards devising a stringent cybersecurity framework. These strengths and weaknesses could vary, including cybersecurity incompetence. In dealing with this weakness, the organization could opt to outsource the cybersecurity function to experts who would help the organization through the concept's development in an organization. The organization could also provide education and training on cybersecurity and undertake a later evaluation to determine the effectiveness of the newly acquired knowledge and skills and whether employees are implementing the same as they discharge their organizational responsibilities. Even after training, cybersecurity incompetence could prompt the organization to lay off employees, especially in technology-based companies, or move them to not technology-intensive departments. If the organization boasts of strength in employing cybersecurity measures, these capabilities should be continually reinforced to the advantage of the employees and organizations. Following the findings, the organization could also increase the resources and funds allocated to cybersecurity.

Forbes Technology Council (2019) highlighted that an organization's examination of strengths and weaknesses creates substantial ground for developing an effective plan. The article highlighted some of the critical areas requiring examination to gauge an organization's strengths and weaknesses. Forbes Technology Council (2019) observed that risk management is all about the dedication of personnel and making security a personal responsibility. An organization's security posture is certainly immature if it is difficult to determine who controls security threats in the firm. Continuous risk assessment and reporting to authorized individuals are among the crucial aspects of cyber risk management. An organization's strength or weakness could be in the form of the organization's cultural risk. A culture of a developed risk culture is an essential indicator of a company's security standpoint. A healthy risk culture encourages all employees to be honest about their encounters and connect risks with strategic objectives. With the absence of a strong risk culture, an organization's decisions could conflict with strategic, tactical, and operational objectives.

VI. Ensuring the implementation of the organizational controls. Hackers and other criminals can be deterred by implementing the proper security controls. However, each form of internal control has its attention. Preventive controls help to avoid incidents and prevent illegal access. Organizations must, however, expand controls outside traditional borders due to technologies to incorporate cloud and remote access. Detective controls assist in the monitoring and alerting of malicious and unauthorized behavior within the organization. Corrective controls are intended to keep the scope of an incident to a minimum and to prevent illegal conduct. These controls could encounter a challenge in implementation in the form of inadequate employee and management support and limited funding. Radvanovsky and McDougall (2013) observed that most organizations tend to have fixed budgets on the protection systems. This budget could limit the organization from fully covering the vulnerabilities imposing risk on data assets. The authors observed that organizations should focus on how the limited financial budgets could be best utilized to provide optimal protection. The protective and corrective controls could incur direct and indirect costs that require consideration during these controls' implementation. IBM Cloud Education (2019) defined security controls as the thresholds put in place to protect various data and infrastructure types crucial to a company. Security control is any safeguard or countermeasure used to prevent, detect, and subvert security risks to information systems, computer networks, or organizational assets. These controls could include penalties for non-compliance to these standards. IBM Cloud Education (2019) observed that these standards could include digital security controls such as a username, strong passwords, and two user authentications. Another standard could be physical security control, including surveillance cameras, access control cards, and intrusion detection systems.

Dr. Tunde Alaofin

PROTECTIONS AND SOLUTIONS
APPLICABLE TO PRIVATE CITIZENS

Cybersecurity is an intricate subject requiring collaboration between the organization, the government, and corporations. The government and corporations should put the right frameworks and invest in resources geared towards cybersecurity. However, the lack of a personal initiative towards cybersecurity could render all efforts fruitless. Every individual should take cybersecurity as a personal responsibility to self, family and friends, community, and the country at large. To individuals, cybersecurity is extremely important as people are increasingly experiencing situations and interacting with devices that could potentially influence cybersecurity. Cellphones, computers, and the internet have become an integral part of modern living, and it is impossible to envision how one might operate without them. Online banking, shopping, email communication, and social media are examples of technologies that have infiltrated human livelihood, making it more critical than ever to take precautions to protect our accounts, data, and gadgets from cybercriminals. IoT adoption and device interoperability have increased dramatically in recent years, creating an insecure ecosystem that is increasingly prone to personal data leakage. The Electronic Privacy Information Center (2021) highlighted cybersecurity as entailing to a set of difficulties aimed at safeguarding digital data and the technologies that enable communication. The Internet is an interconnected world of computers that presents new problems for governments due to regional or national borders' inability to control the flow of information. The Internet functions similarly to any other remote addressing system in its most basic form, such as how a phone number relates to a specific device. The following are individual controls geared towards ensuring cybersecurity.

I. Avoid oversharing on social media. People can be carried in the heat of the moment and want to readily share ever-exciting information with their family and friends on social media. However, not everybody in social media is who they claim to be. The information could include a new job opportunity, date of birth, admission letters, among others. While the information is worth sharing, it puts an individual at risk of identity theft. Invasion of computer systems and networks, and data tampering. Most information such as birth dates are often used as passwords to crucial steps, giving cybercriminals an easy pass. Social media invites users to share more information about themselves to create matching profiles of friends with similar interests, residing from the same country and even community. These platforms create the urge to share due to the perceptions about the lives other people lead. As portrayed on social media profiles, other people's lives can give the idea of the lives of others being so much better. People can easily get a glimpse of the lives of others more than they did in the past. People may check on and look at other people's vacation images, then wonder why their lives are so monotonous. As a result, they may feel insecure about their own life. They may feel compelled to post their own best times whenever possible to outdo their friends and appear remarkably interesting. Tagging locations during these posts create real-life and cybersecurity concerns. In most cases, the images on social media are a misrepresentation of the real-life of these users. Thatcher et al. (2018) noted that recently, there had been concerns about gathering, analyzing, and utilizing information provided on social media. Despite the information being used in marketing initiatives, it could be used in creating profiles and committing crimes that could cause reputational damage to the real identity owner. When sharing information online, social media users should use privacy settings that limit information access to only individuals the user is sure of their identity.

II. Hold conversations with family and friends on online security and safety. Internet could be overwhelming and a new thing for some children, hence the importance of conversations surrounding online safety and security. These conversations should give insights into some of the online norms that jeopardize an individual's safety. Most people embrace basic aspects that potentially increase their vulnerability while using computers, among other devices, to access the internet. Parents and guardians would need to determine the best time to initiate conversations on online safety. In the modern world, children are starting to use the internet at a younger age. With the embraced remote learning following the onset of the COVID-19, these children are bound to lead cybercriminals to their world innocently. Eliciting the possibility of their confidential information being stolen or being cyberbullied. School-aged children are increasingly obtaining online independence and could go online unsupervised, facing greater internet safety hazards than younger children. The concern is more when children use social media and games to communicate with each other. Their innocence may make them easily fall to the bait of adults masquerading as their age mates. These children should be accustomed to age-friendly platforms and content and use child-friendly search engines like YouTube kids.

III. Citizens should embrace the use of antivirus as part of personal protection measures. The National Cybersecurity Center (n.d) highlighted antivirus (AV) software as software types involved in detecting and blocking viruses from running on computers. AV collaborates with network defenses, device configuration, and app store in blocking malware before it can cause any harm. Malware infection, including ransomware, is one of the common ways of compromising IT systems. National Cybersecurity Center (n, d) noted that malware infection could result in data loss, ransom payments for data recovery, and disruption of provided services. AV use is one of the many ways of infection prevention. The National Cybersecurity Center (n.d) noted that the operations of the AV software involve the scanning of the files maintained in a device and looking for malware through the identification of new signatures.

IV. Change strong passwords regularly. Home Wi-Fi networks should have strong passwords that are changed often. The password to the Wi-Fi network keeps hackers and other intruders from gaining access to one's home wireless network, stealing bandwidth, and keeping track of communications. One prefers a password that's simple enough to offer to visitors who want to access your wireless network, but hackers can easily crack a simple and weak password. Equipment manufacturers and broadband service providers often set up a router with a secure password in many instances. In some cases, the password could be the device's serial number, written on the router's bottom label. However, it is always important to choose a fresh password when you initially receive the device for the best security and ensure a continued password change within a given period. Like any other password, a Wi-Fi password is preferred to go for a stronger password for maximum security experience. A strong password is a gateway to secure passwords. Manoj (2020) highlighted strong passwords as one of the cybersecurity countermeasures or controls aimed at reducing or mitigating the potential of risk occurrence. Countermeasures could include configuration to eliminate the possibility of a threat agent that could exploit an underlying vulnerability. However, a strong password for secure Wi-Fi does not necessarily mean going for complex passwords. Spellman and Stoudt (2011) observed that complex, among other string passwords, do not necessarily translate to preventing unauthorized access in control systems. The authors observed that one of the probable reasons is that complex passwords could hinder rapid response during emergencies. On the other hand, weak passwords are easy to guess and share and are often infrequently shared despite their commonality in the control systems.

Small mistakes users make when connecting devices to a network or setting up a router are routinely exploited by Wi-Fi hackers. Few simple steps could be taken to avoid falling prey to some of the most prevalent Wi-Fi attacks. Datplan (2019) sensitized the importance of appropriately securing Wi-Fi points and ensuring that only known devices connect. Security scanning tools should be used in detecting and locating unauthorized wireless access points. Datplan (2019) observed that any provided corporate Wi-Fi should be separated from the public Wi-Fi.

V.   Be cautious of deceptive emails and web pages. People need to be cautious of deceptive messages and webpages links sent through the technique referred to as phishing. Phishing is an umbrella term referring to different online scams to obtain personal and information from online users. The deceptive messages are purported to be from a trusted source, such as a well-known software firm, an online payment provider, a bank, or another trustworthy organization. Some will utilize an organization's email address, logo, and other identifying aspects to ensure credibility and more chances of being believed. Phishing emails may seem to be sent from a family member or friend one trusts. Before falling prey to the emails

and URLs, it is worth taking a key not to examine the identifying aspects that would be proof of identity. However, legitimate links could also be used during a phishing attempt. Many attackers try to avoid detection by email filters by including legitimate links in their phishing emails. They could do so by supplying authentic contact information for the organization they're pretending to be.

People become victims of deceptive emails for not being extra cautious when using the internet. Gonzalez and Kemp (2019) observed that people misunderstand the aftermath of online actions. The author termed the tendency of clicking without thinking as cyber-risk beliefs. These beliefs are often inaccurate, leading to various cyberattack and cyberterrorism incidences. Gonzalez and Kemp (2019) noted that some people believe that their inability to manipulate PDF documents emanates from the stringent cybersecurity measures and open the documents without being wary of the possible risk. The flawed beliefs of the inability to circumvent the sophisticated technologies also propel others to open webpages and receive attachments from their mobile devices while using some operating systems. The email and social media habits coupled with the highlighted beliefs also increase susceptibility to attacks. Habits refer to the brain's mods of automation due to repeated acts, resulting in predictive behaviors. Gonzalez and Kemp (2019) observed that as time passes by, checking emails and social media platforms become a routine, and people might become unaware of the reasons for committing such acts. While in the spirit of encouraging the behavior, a person could end up unconsciously opening a deceptive email, attachment, or webpage. Access to mobile devices catalyzes the outlined habitual reactions. Gonzalez and Kemp (2019) observed that these devices ensure quick and reactive responses to messages through apps and push notifications. The compressed layouts in applications provide easy access to emails while concealing lots of information that could help single out an email as deceptive.

VI.   Avoid using public Wi-Fi. Public Wi-Fi access points have been a strategy used by many organizations and government corporations to ensure they remain engaged while awaiting services. Nothing that comes for free is completely safe, and people should be extra careful when using free public Wi-Fi. Hackers pose a threat to Wi-Fi users. However, there are protections in place that users should exploit before freely using these networks. Working professionals have significantly benefited from the recent boom of free public Wi-Fi. Since these free access sites may be found at restaurants, bookstores, and even random retail establishments, people are remarkably close to accessing their work network and preparing before heading to work. However, this independence comes with a cost, and few people know the dangers of using public Wi-Fi. Your vital company data will be safe if you learn how to protect yourself. Using public Wi-Fi, especially when accessing crucial networks with confidential information, increase the possibility of compromising an entire computer system, resulting in data loss. The reasons that make the public WIFI preferable among citizens encourage the network's utilization, which is the lack of authentication. A hacker using this network has a considerable opportunity to infiltrate unsecured devices on the same network. Hackers could use the free connections as a gateway to spread malware. Most people maintain personal information on their mobile devices, including their social security numbers, bank account numbers, and date of births. This information could be used to conduct many cyber-crimes, including identity theft and data tampering. Miller and Meinzinger (2016) observed that unsecured networks should not be used in exchanging confidential information. Cyber-criminals could use scanners to intercept calls from unsecured devices using public Wi-Fi. Ballew (2011) advised users to avoid inputting sensitive information while on an open network and ensure keyboard coverage when keying in passwords, credit numbers, and social security numbers.

PROTECTIONS AND SOLUTIONS APPLICABLE TO EDUCATIONAL AND HEALTHCARE INSTITUTIONS

T he drastic increase in remote learning following the COVID-19 pandemic has resulted in a surge in cyberattack incidents. As a result, employing cyber protections and solution is a necessity and not an option. The protective measures may differ from one institution depending on the population, demographic characteristics, technology reliance, resources, and infrastructure. Cybersecurity attacks in health institutions are detrimental to the patient's health and wellbeing. A patient could die, or their health could deteriorate due to the inability to access healthcare services during a cyberattack. The cyberattacks targeting health institutions significantly impact operations and are scary. A crucial and life-saving surgery could be derailed due to the inability to locate essential information such as the patient's blood type following a cyberattack. The following are the basic considerations that education and healthcare institutions could put in place. However, while one option could be effective in healthcare, it could be ineffective in education and vice versa.

I. Security training. The educational sector is increasingly becoming a target for cybercriminals. Security awareness training is one of the possible efforts to equip the staff and students on preventive measures and loopholes to avoid ensuring cybersecurity. The COVID-19 pandemic has forced most learning institutions to adopt the remote learning model without being prepared for the same. As a result, teachers and students that were not used to the technological infrastructure have been forced by circumstances to learn them. The simple aspects are those that could end up compromising an institution's cybersecurity. Students are exposed to digital hacks and bugs when they log on to attend online classes. Public hotspots for schools with a free Wi-Fi system could be easily hacked or cloned, giving hackers access to thousands of students' and staff's laptops and mobile devices. Educational systems hold vast student information databases, including personal information such as birth certificates, addresses, phone numbers, medical records, and even biometrics. A single breach of a school's computer system might expose over a thousand people. Cybersecurity measures in schools cannot measure up to those in corporations; something hackers can exploit.

Similarly, health institutions have become overly busy, especially with the influence of admissions due to the COVID-19 pandemic. Most workers in healthcare institutions have training on healthcare services provision and may not be well versed with cybersecurity knowledge. However, these skills and competence are particularly important as these medical provisions interact with computer systems when retrieving or storing patients' medical information.

Considering the ever-changing cybercriminal techniques, security training would be imperative to equip healthcare workers, teachers, non-teaching staff, and students with skills and knowledge to identify social engineering and phishing attempts. Wu et al. (2020) highlighted that security awareness programs provide security requirements, policies, and guidelines in ensuring information security in an institution. This training would inform the highlighted individuals on crucial aspects to adhere to, such as what to do when using computer networks, password development, and identifying possibilities of cyberattacks. The training would also eliminate the general ignorance on cybersecurity and eliminate the simple mistakes individuals in these institutions make that compromise computer systems, networks, and confidential information.

II. Cybersecurity framework. This protective solution could be effective for both health and education institutions. The cybersecurity framework ensures an entity has a united front in the mitigation of cyber risks. A cybersecurity framework is a set of best practices that a company should follow to manage its cybersecurity risk. The framework's purpose is to lower the company's vulnerability to cyberattacks and to identify areas most vulnerable to data breaches and other compromising actions by cybercriminals. The framework also ensures that every individual in the institution has a similar understanding of what is required of them as far as cybersecurity is concerned. The framework would also help highlight the crucial areas of prioritization depending on the institution in question. For instance, healthcare institutions could identify the most computer systems that require extra caution due to the nature of stored information. Characteristically, the frameworks could help determine the password measures for the two institutions depending on the stored data. These measures could highlight the password strength and the frequency of changing the passwords. The cybersecurity framework should be considerate of the institutions' risk management strategy. If developed and implemented with the seriousness it deserves, the framework could help guide the affected individuals and safeguard them from a considerable proportion of cyber risk. This framework is crucial as most cyberattacks occur due to mistakes and omissions that could be avoided. The framework should also highlight punitive measures for individuals failing to adhere to guidelines. The punitive measures gear towards compliance and ensuring the desired level of seriousness applies.

III. Installation of anti-malware and antivirus software: Healthcare and education institutions should install anti-virus and anti-malware software and ensure that they are routinely updated alongside other software in the computer systems. Hackers exploit weaknesses presented by outdated software in ensuring access to computer systems and networks. The highlighted software protects from malicious attacks through viruses and malware. Malware detection helps protect the system while providing adequate information on subverting similar attacks in the future. The antivirus does not solely protect against virus attacks as denoted by its name. It also protects from malware. Ensuring that the institutions have the two software helps each play a complementary role and strengthen cybersecurity.

IV. Threat identification and assessment. Adequate and proper planning in ensuring cybersecurity and providing protection eventually. The assessment would also facilitate the development of systems to safeguard from the occurrence of cyber incidents that could potentially cripple an organization and cause significant physical and emotional harm. Generally, identifying and assessing threats becomes the initial step of healthcare and education institutions' cybersecurity decisions. The threat identification procedure looks at IT flaws and evaluates how dangerous they are to your system. It's an essential part of your company's risk management strategy. Detecting dangers allows your company to take preventative measures. This process should also be coupled with the Cybersecurity risk assessment. The process of risk discovery, analysis, and evaluation is known as Cybersecurity risk assessment. The process aids in ensuring that selected Cybersecurity measures are appropriate for the threats facing a given entity. Much time, money, and effort could go to waste due to the absence of a risk assessment to guide Cybersecurity decisions. It is pointless to put safeguards against situations that are unlikely to occur or have no bearing on an operation.

During the risk assessment, evaluation and risk estimation are undertaken, followed by selecting controls to counter the identified risks. It is critical to continuously monitor and assess the risk environment to detect any changes in the organization's context and keep track of the entire risk management process. The risk assessment process could be different for the health and education institutions. However, there are fundamental aspects that the two entities could consider. A regular risk assessment entails the determination of the various information assets that a cyberattack could harm. The assets could include teachers, staff, students' information, patients' information, hardware, computer systems, etc. The assessment should also cover the numerous threats that could harm those assets. After undertaking the risk assessment and evaluation, what follows is the selection of controls to address the identified risks. It is critical to continuously monitor and assess the risk environment to detect any changes in the organization's context and keep track of the entire risk management process. The risk assessment should be a continuous process. Romancheva (2021) highlighted the ever-changing nature and speed of cyber risks. Therefore, the results of a risk assessment could be redundant later. Kavallieratos and Katsikas (2020) highlighted STRIDE risk assessment as informed by the threats of spoofing, tampering, repudiation, information disclosure, denial of service, and elevation of privileges.

V. Cybersecurity champion. This protection could require the healthcare and education institution to identify individuals who buy the dream of ensuring cybersecurity, have a foresight of its positive impact eventually, and sell the dream to other individuals to initiate a positive attitude and acceptance. Like in any organization, an initiative's success depends on its reception and the employees' attitudes. People who readily accept an invention would ensure commitment towards its achievement and influence others to follow through. Ensuring cybersecurity is a change process for the health and education institutions, especially with the unavailability of seriousness in an institution. As an intricate issue, the institutions need to ensure that all people are in and committed to ensuring the change's success. Deriving this commitment could necessitate the involvement of the various stakeholders. Involvement could be in the form of communicating the awaiting change and portraying the importance of the change for the wellbeing of the employees, the clientele base, and the long-term operations of an entity. Resistance to change is a common challenge that could characterize the adoption of cybersecurity. Some could be uncooperative due to the fear of the unknown. Charoensukmongkol (2017) observed that resistance to change is a multidimensional construct comprising attitude, feelings towards change, and perception of change. As a result, adequate communication would gear towards changing attitudes, perceptions, and feelings towards cybersecurity, with people embracing the mindset of cybersecurity as geared towards the best. The institutions could utilize incentives during the change introduced as a means of encouraging the acceptance of the introduced measures.

TECHNOLOGIES FOR CYBERSECURITY ENHANCEMENT

Cybercrime masterminds frequently exhibit technological prowess comparable to that of their Cybersecurity colleagues. This has resulted in a continually changing panorama of cybercrime that outsmarts modern Cybersecurity technologies. The bone of contention is whether the tug of war between cybercriminals and cybersecurity experts is the end of the efforts targeting cyber threats. The solution is to raise awareness and employ advanced Cybersecurity solutions. Technology advances rapidly, and hackers are always one step ahead of or familiar with the technology, allowing them to breach it quickly. Malware, a software assault, or threats to your system are all sorts of attacks. Hackers and cybercriminals are becoming more sophisticated by the hour or minute. Their amazing approaching techniques deceive people. Continually, individuals, government agencies, and citizens encounter threats that cannot be entirely solved by available software, necessitating the adoption of cybersecurity technologies as the mitigating strategy. The following are the technologies to consider in cybersecurity.

I.   Machine Learning

Machine learning is a subset of artificial intelligence that predicts a computer's behavior using algorithms derived from prior datasets and statistical analysis. The computer can then adapt its behavior — and even accomplish tasks for which it was not specifically intended. Cybersecurity systems can look for trends and learn from them to prevent future attacks and adjust to changing behavior. It can assist cybersecurity teams in being proactive during threats prevention and making a swift response to live attacks. It can help firms use their resources more strategically by reducing time spent on regular tasks. Sarkar et al. (2020) highlighted that machine learning, a key component of artificial intelligence (AI), can help uncover new insights from data. Machine learning has the potential to drastically alter the cybersecurity landscape, with data science being at the forefront of a new scientific paradigm. Machine learning could potentially make cybersecurity more easy, proactive, cost-efficient, and successful. However, it can only do so if the underlying data used to inform machine learning provide a comprehensive view of the environment. Aiyanyo et al. (2020) observed that machine learning provides offensive and defensive solutions in handling massive data amounts and using complex detection logic that would be impossible when relying on traditional techniques. This technology relies on the computer concept of garbage in, garbage out. In machine learning, the most vital thing is focusing on data as the key point to ensuring cybersecurity.

Machine learning is the process of creating patterns and modifying them using algorithms. A lot of rich data is needed from all over the place to generate patterns since the data needs to represent as many possible outcomes from as many different circumstances as possible. It is not just about the amount of available data. It is also about how good it is. Whether at the endpoint, on the network, or in the cloud, every possible source must provide a complete, relevant, and rich context for the data. It is important to clean the data to make sense of the collected information and identified results. Thanks to its ability to go through millions of data and identify potentially infected ones, machine learning is increasingly being used as a means of detecting dangers and automatically eliminating them before they can cause destruction.

Organizations could have invested in machine learning and put all the required infrastructures in place but failed to enjoy the benefits through reinforced cybersecurity fully. It all narrows down to the collected data. The obtained information must include details about everything that occurred, not just the threats to the computer systems and networks. The data must be comprehensive enough to provide information on machines, applications, protocols, and network sensors. It must provide a link between what is seen on the network and what is evident at the endpoint. Machine learning could be utilized in collaboration with other cybersecurity techniques. Haider et al. (2021) highlighted the capabilities of a new intrusion detection system (IDS) in managing cyber threats to computer networks or systems. An IDS recognizes security weaknesses and difficulties by detecting adverse cyberattack actions on a system while recording and reviewing daily operations in a system and the information structure. The demand for information security has recently risen, necessitating protection from a variety of threats. Unwanted device activity such as unauthorized entry, tampering, or disturbance is frequently tracked, monitored, and classified by an IDS. Haider et al. (2021) highlighted the infusion of an efficient detection system with machine learning to mitigate problems of manipulating existing and unknown flaws and cyberattacks.

When using machine learning, part of the requirement is consolidating all that data to get a perfect scenario of the entire situation. The step that could follow is the development of different models with different element behaviors and use algorithms to decide when to caution the team, when to act in responding to potential risks, and when to come up with protective measures depending on the comprehensive situational analysis. Every entity has its business aspect, which is the desired impact and derived benefits in the form of improved earnings. As a result, the incorporation of machine learning in cybersecurity should capitalize on the business aspect by imposing the right measures to ensure the right aspects are in place. An entity should determine the possession of the correct data in ensuring an adequate response towards the identified cyber risks. However, meeting the data requirement does not necessarily mean any form of information. Instead, the organization should gear towards data quality to derive the most efficient and effective efforts to mitigate identified risks.

Machine learning has gone through significant changes, a process bound to continue even in the past. Halder and Ozdemir (2018) highlighted the prominence of machine learning in the 1980s following the success of artificial neural networks (ANNs). This technology was much applauded in the 1990s following the researchers; reliance on this technology in the resolution of challenges characterizing the daily livelihood. In the 2000s, the internet and digitization intensified machine learning, with companies such as Google and Amazon relying on machine learning to manage human-computer interactions. The intensified cybersecurity and cyberattack complexities have created several avenues for machine learning to resolve the imposed challenges. Halder and Ozdemir (2018) highlighted ace recognition as one of the domains resolved under machine learning. The face recognition systems can determine people from digital images through recognition of facial features. The authors observed that machine learning could also detect fake news. Fake news has been so rampant, to the point of infiltrating serious concerns such as the 2016 United States presidential elections. The fake news detectors rely on semantic and stylistic patterns of the article's text to differentiate them from the original news articles. Halder and Ozdemir (2018) highlighted machine learning as enabling recommender and fraud detection systems. Recommender systems can determine a customer's choice and preference depending on the customer's history of choices. The popularity of these systems emanates from their utilization by industries in making sales. On the other hand, the fraud detection systems would mitigate risks and safety fraud depending on a customer's interests.

II.   Artificial Intelligence

Artificial intelligence is the future of cybersecurity. According to IBM (hh), Artificial intelligence (AI) assists security operations analysts with resource challenges in staying ahead of threats as cyberattacks increase in volume and become more complex. AI technologies like machine learning and natural language processing derive their threat intelligence from millions of research papers and news stories, providing instant insights to cut through the bother emanating from the noise of daily alerts and substantially lowering response times. Artificial intelligence is an attempt to mimic human intelligence. It has enormous potential in the field of cybersecurity. Artificial Intelligence (AI) systems can be trained to provide threat warnings, identify new malware types, and protect critical data for businesses if used correctly. As the name depicts, AI is all about intelligence, with the technology utilizing the intelligence to reinforce network security over time. It learns the behavior of a business network over time using machine learning and deep learning. AI detects patterns in the network and consolidates them. This technology then explores any deviations or security issues from the norm before acting. Artificial neural networks can assist in improving security in the future by learning patterns over time. Potential threats with identical characteristics to those documented are identified early enough and stopped. The fact that AI is in a constant learning mode makes it harder for hackers to outsmart it. Artificial intelligence bypasses human intelligence in cybersecurity in numerous ways. A human being may not be able to recognize all a company's dangers. Annually, hackers carry out hundreds of millions of attacks for a variety of reasons. Unknown threats can do a lot of harm to a network. Even worse is the damage they can cause if they are not discovered, identified, and prevented in time. As attackers' experiment with new strategies, such as sophisticated social engineering and malware attacks, contemporary solutions are needed to protect against them.

AI has been shown to be one of the most effective technologies for identifying and preventing unexpected dangers from wreaking havoc on a corporation. Das and Sandhane (2021) observed that many government departments, businesses, and private sector companies have already deployed AI programs. The White House wondered about the government department's adoption of the technology. AI goes through standardized data and thoroughly understands and studies unstructured data, numbers, voice patterns, and words. AI may quickly save resources and time. In reality, AI has the potential to save both tax dollars and national secrets. However, like any other technology, AI has gaps. Hackers are attempting to gain access to the devices by sliding through holes people never knew existed. During a cyberattack, and in the absence of AI, a hacker can easily infiltrate a system, and by the time the organization learns about the ordeal, the hacker would be long gone. However, Das and Sandhane 2021) noted that with artificial intelligence (AI), they silently collect data until a mess occurs following the hackers' antics. The article noted that AI is on the lookout for behavior anomalies to depict. Such as when a user login into a system. The AI flags off patterns that could be humanly impossible to detect and derail the occurrence of a cyberattack. The hackers exploit any weaknesses in a computer system, and with AI being human controlled, they could wrap their way around it. Das and Sandhane (2021) observed that despite the remarkable ability of AI to connect and process data, it could function as much as it was formulated to do. During the hackers'' adjustment of the AI systems, the programmers release defense measures. As the cat and mouse chase continues, AI positively strengthens the fight in securing data.

As a computer science discipline, AI uses conventional computer programs to simulate human intelligence. This century's three key scientific and technical achievements are AI as a developing comprehensive marginal discipline, atomic energy technology, and space technology. AI is currently evolving into a massive technological system. Sun et al. (2019) observed that machine learning, deep learning, human-computer interaction, natural language processing, and machine vision are all examples of AI technologies. AI has made significant strides in the network security field. The first instance is the big data analysis utilization in dangers identification and the creation of large-scale security systems based on big data. The second instance is an examination of associated security postures, which includes a thorough understanding of internal and external security threats. Sun et al. (2019) observed that the third option is a self-learning emergency reaction defense system that can create an active security defense system. In recent years, multi-agent systems, neural networks, expert systems, machine learning, and other artificial intelligence technologies have made their way into network security defense. However, the authors discovered a scarcity of relevant research on penetration testing in artificial intelligence.

The advantages of utilizing AI in cybersecurity reinforcement have been depicted in several, ways. The first instance is through the utilization of technology in the penetration of testing systems. Currently, manual penetration testing is widely relied on in power grid enterprise vulnerability assessment and verification operations. In recent years, there has been an evolution in the never-ending flood of network security attack technologies. Sun et al. (2019) observed that power grid firms are increasingly investing in a significant amount of labor in penetration tester training to minimize grid security threats and ensure the safe and steady operation of power grids. Despite the availability of financial resources, these power grids cannot meet the enterprise needs of network security problems. However, infusing AI into penetration testing systems could help in the resolution of several challenges. The first is that AI could compensate for personnel shortages. Sun et al. (2019) observed that the low degree of artificial penetration automation couples with the high personnel demand. The increased cyberattacks result in increased degrees of harm and the growing demand for corporate network security professionals. The article highlighted that the automated penetration testing system could compensate for the personnel shortages.

Efficiencies also create avenues for cyberattacks, and artificial intelligence (AI) improves work efficiency and enhances cybersecurity while at it. Sun et al. (2019) observed that artificial penetration testing is inefficient and time-consuming. This is the trend while considering the underlying factors such as the surge in the emerging cyberattacks and the growing complexities of the current network environment. In the face of the big data volumes, the amount of data processed by network security penetration testers cannot match the processing capacity. However, Sun et al. (2019) noted that network security risks could improve significantly through capitalizing on intelligent models to verify vulnerabilities.

III. Blockchain Technology

No technology is 100% secure in providing a safe online environment, safe computer systems and networks, and reducing the risk of cyberattacks and the negative effects that could be associated with the same. Today, what could be considered a safe technology could not be considered the same in months to come due to its attractiveness. Blockchain is increasingly popular in mitigating emerging cyber risks, despite the underlying criticisms of suitability, sustainability, and security. Mentsiev et al. (2019) observed that Blockchains are decentralized networks that link millions of people worldwide. Cryptography is used to secure all the data that each user contributes to the Blockchain. Every Blockchain member contributes to the Blockchain's security by verifying every piece of data uploaded to the Blockchain. This is accomplished by using three keys: a private key, a public key, and a receiver's key. This verification allows Blockchain users to check the authenticity of data, but it also allows them to confirm the data source.

The Blockchain formation adheres to a complex process, and a piece of information cannot be just added to the Blockchain. The addition requires the conversion of the information to a block. In undertaking the conversion, Blockchain users rely on their keys and strong computing engines in running algorithms to resolve complex problems. Mentsiev et al. (2019) observed that there is the creation of a block following the successful resolution of a problem. The block is then added to the Blockchain, where it remains forever unchanged. Sidi 9GGG) observed that Blockchain technology 9BCT) initially appeared in 2008 through Bitcoin use. BCT is part of disruptive technologies perceived to be the means of revolutionizing and modifying the industry's future. The article observed that BCT's creation aimed to ensure autonomy, speed, and efficiency for factories with a smart and digital connection. Weidong et el. (2020) noted that Blockchain provides a decentralized mechanism and infrastructure in various fields as the technology behind Bitcoin. This technology provides a continuous chronology of the data that also remains unhampered. The author observed that when the real and digital word assets develop digital assets, the Blockchain technology becomes the perfect fit to assert class while providing a digital proof of ownership and timestamps. This attribute makes the Blockchain applicable in various fields involving online payments, stock exchange, and trade management. According to Weidong et al. (2020), Blockchain technology is the technology foundation of all cryptocurrencies and provides applications to traditional finances and trade.

The evolving nature of cyberattacks has necessitated the consideration of other cybersecurity technologies, including Blockchain. Hackers use diverse strategies in their infiltration of the cyber network, including phishing attacks through imitation of Wi-Fi networks or a program that could prompt a login attempt from the employees of organizations, and the hackers end up obtaining the login credentials. Despite the type of hacking strategy, a cybercriminal uses, it all narrows down to consolidating and storing data in a single location. When hackers obtain the location, they could either steal the data or manipulate the owners and users for ransom payments. Mentsiev et al. (2019) highlighted that Blockchain alters the data storage narrative by decentralizing data storage. The Blockchain alters the entire dynamic of protecting networks from cyberattacks through decentralization. The article highlighted Blockchain as ensuring data decentralization instead of being gathered from a common access point where it can easily be hacked or stolen by hackers. Instead, this technology preserves data in large data farms containing servers or even in massive cloud storage. Blockchain also disintegrates every data piece or transaction into small pieces and shares it along with the network. Mentsiev et al. (2019) observed that since the networks are associated with millions of users at a given time, the Blockchain, could at a given time, have millions of servers referred to as 'nodes' Each node acts as a storage for each transaction chunk and a transaction to take place, these nodes come together to form a complete piece of information. If any node is hacked or taken down, it will not affect data as it will remain intact. Sidi et al. (2020 highlighted the potential of Blockchain technology (BCT) in enhancing cybersecurity. Particularly with the decentralized distribution network aimed at deriving trust in an entirely untrusted network involving unknown individuals.

Depending on the people who can access the BTC network and the accorded permissions in writing the BCT network, there exist four BCT types. Sidi et al. (2020) noted that public BCTs are accessible by the public, and anyone can participate in them in undertaking transactions. These BCTs rely on proof of work (PoW) and proof of stake (PoS). This technology stood as a better preference concerning cybersecurity issues. Compared to other technologies, BCT provides a better guarantee of an effective cost through the exploitation of traceability and non-repudiation. Blockchain technology also fosters cybersecurity by facilitating peer-to-peer sharing. Mentisev et al. (2019) highlighted this form of sharing as involving the sharing of data by one user with the same received by one recipient through the reliance on the million nodes on the network and keys given to the two Blockchain users. Peer-to-peer sharing ensures that data is not gathered or shared through a single network. This sharing makes the Blockchain take the position of the middleman during the sharing process. One user shares data or a transaction through the widely distributed Blockchain network, with the receiver using a unique key without the knowledge of a third party.

IV. Content-Aware Behavior Analysis

This is the programming system that analyzes or monitors the undertaken actions in each platform. This application is used by Facebook, Instagram, and other social media networks to match users with individuals matching their characteristics and while utilizing the provided information. The technology keeps track of what you like and preferences and what you do and don't do. This analysis facilitates the identification and location of possible threats. This system receives a notification if there is any unusual activity. Many businesses have adopted it since it has proven to be one of the most effective cybersecurity technologies to date. Palomares et al. (2017) highlighted that content-aware behavior analytics involves content-aware technologies availing application mechanisms to foster the adaptation to the changing contexts and alter the behaviors depending on the user requirements. Palomares et al. (2017) gave the example of smart homes with context-aware applications that can alert an individual's hospital requiring urgent medical attention. Zhiwen et al. (2019) highlighted the Context-Aware Anomaly Behavior Analysis System (CA-ABAS) for the protection of smart home systems (SHS). The article highlighted that CA-ABAS is a form of intrusion detection framework protecting SHS from known and unknown cyberattacks.

An intrusion detection software (IDS) plays an instrumental role in the efforts geared towards reinforcing cybersecurity. Pascale et al. (2021) observed that IDS is a hardware or software system striving to detect any form of acts that could potentially compromise the confidentiality, integrity, and availability of data resources. These systems are classified into primary types depending on the intrusion detection strategy. The signature detection involves comparing the collected data against known attacks while looking for correspondence that would ascertain the presence of an occurring attack. Anomaly detection involves monitoring the system's behavior to ensure that the methods do not stray from everyday use. Content-Aware Behavior Analysis is part of the content-aware technologies that could effectively foster cybersecurity in institutions, corporations, governments, and private citizens. The possibility of a rise of context-aware security was predicted as an emerging option for businesses to react to changing security landscapes such as cloud computing and the ever-changing threat landscape.

Content-aware security involves using extra data to improve security judgments at the point of decision-making, yielding more accurate security decisions that can support dynamic business and IT environments. Sarker et al. (2020) highlighted the recent advancement of attributes such as IoT devices, including smartphones, as their effectiveness in daily lives and improved quality of life. Voice communication is the primary function of mobile devices. However, people use smartphones for other daily activities while using apps such as social media, location tracking, and instant messaging. The article highlighted the ever-changing behaviors of users when using these applications, with the differences exhibited from one user to another depending on their current needs. Content-aware security measures could facilitate the development of technologies and strategies to safeguard from cyberattacks through reliance on content rules. Sarker (2019) highlighted context-aware rules aimed at developing rule-based intelligent context-aware systems. According to the article, the context-aware contains two parts: If & Then. The antecedent part denotes the contextual information surrounding a user, including temporal and social contexts. The consequent part (Then) denotes the corresponding behavior or activities as motivated by the initial part. Sarker (2019) highlighted the reliance on advanced data analysis while utilizing machine learning techniques for effective and efficient decision-making n different context-aware circumstances.

V.   Firewall

A firewall refers to a network security device that monitors and sieves through the flow in network traffic while adhering to security regulations set by an organization. A firewall is a barricade that separates a private internal network from the public Internet. The primary goal of a firewall is to allow non-threatening traffic while eliminating harmful traffic. A cybersecurity firewall could be a network or software. In an organizational setting, every employee could have a wired or wireless interface allowing the connection to the organization's network. The organization could have several connections to the internet. In the absence of a firewall, all the devices connected to the network are vulnerable to different attacks from the attackers and could be communicating to attackers who may be masquerading as co-workers. A firewall is a preventive measure against attackers targeting to exploit security vulnerabilities. The organization creates a firewall for every connection with the internet. Stewart (2020) highlighted that not all connections are from an authorized source and should not be given an easy chance to join and exit the company network. Additional networks might not be for an authorized purpose and should be blocked before accessing the targeted destinations. The firewalls provide all the highlighted protections. As the name depicts, a firewall is a tool aimed at derailing damage, just as it occurs in a firewall in an engine compartment to protect passengers in a vehicle due to harm emanating from an accident. Stewart (2020) defined a firewall as a hardware device, or a software product deployed to enforce an access control policy in network communications. As a result, a firewall is a filter to eliminate data messages and harmful exploitations in network traffic.

The positioning of the firewalls is essential as far as cybersecurity is concerned. Firewalls are located at the edge of a network or subnet to protect from the various threats emanating from internet use. Firewalls protect the throughput or bandwidth in a private network so that resources are only availed to authorized users.

Mahfouz (2020) highlighted firewalls as part of the signature-based detection techniques. Like any other protection technology, firewalls could be potentially infiltrated by external attacks. While the signature-based techniques provide defense from known attacks, they cannot detect zero-day attacks. Characteristically, they do not provide an adequate safeguard from skilled attackers relying on recent attack techniques that can easily evade such security controls.

Firewall installations could also be dependent on an organization's operations. Firewalls can also be installed on client and server computers. Stewart (2020) noted that host software firewalls could safeguard a single host from threats posed by internet use, in addition to the threats from the network and other internal network elements. The firewall configuration is for the traffic control based on the deny-by-default/allow-by-exception stand. As a result, nothing passes through the network just because it is in the network. Therefore, all the traffic reaching the firewall must fulfill the requirements of progressing on its path. Stewart (2020) noted that the IT professional chooses to determine the allowed traffic to pass through the firewalls or the blocked traffic. Also, one can determine whether the filtering occurs on inbound traffic (ingress filtering), outbound traffic (egress filtering), or both. Filtering inbound traffic is an essential component due to most threats occurring outside the network, which also necessitates outbound filtering.

SUMMARY

Cyberattacks pose significant threats to corporations, governments, private citizens, healthcare, and education institutions. Compromised networks and computer systems due to hacking could result in reputational damage and service disruptions. The case is worse for health care facilities as such attacks could derail service provision, making it difficult to make medical prescriptions and initiate treatment. These disruptions are detrimental to patients' healthcare and wellbeing and could result in death or worsening health conditions. Leaked information could compromise a patient's health status, especially if such a person holds a prominent position in society. The COVID-19 pandemic has resulted in a growing surge in cyberattacks. These attacks are associated with fee time people have, making them spend more time online. Characteristically, disruption in education programs has resulted in the drastic adoption of remote learning without adequate measures to safeguard from cyberattacks. Some of the common cyberattacks include malware, phishing, and ransomware. The theft of confidential information could propel citizens and corporations to pay ransom to avoid leaked information to the internet.

Malware injection into the system could result in compromised information and data theft. Phishing attacks could emanate from network users clicking attachments and links without verifying their source. Cybercriminals often use emails from credible organizations during phishing attacks. Most cyberattacks are elegant from the absence of security measures. Companies continue using outdated software and have no stringent network protection measures.

Employees and network users do not have skills and competencies on the internet and network users and end up compromising confidential information and resulting in financial losses. Cyberattacks can cripple critical infrastructure systems such as power grids and water systems. Preventive measures should include the formulation of a cybersecurity framework and cybersecurity awareness training and education. Cybersecurity technologies such as machine learning and artificial intelligence could come in handy in preventing cyberattacks targeting computer systems and networks. The preventive measure could help reduce financial losses, disruption of service provision, reputational damage, and crippled critical infrastructures due to cyberattacks.

REFERENCES

Abeyratne, R. (2011). Cyberterrorism and aviation--national and international responses. *Journal of Transportation Security, 4*(4), 337-349. https://doi.org/10.1007/s12198-011-0074-3

Afshani, J. (2019). Cyberterrorism and its dramatic impact on insurance and security companies. *Journal of Finance and Investment Analysis, 8*(4).

Agboola, A. O. (2015). Neoclassical economics and new institutional economics: An assessment of their methodological implication for property market analysis. *Property Management, 33*(5), 412. https://doi.org/10.1108/PM-12-2014-0055

Ahanger, T. A. (2018). Defense scheme to protect IoT from cyberattacks using AI principles. *International Journal of Computers, Communications, and Control, 13*(6), 915-926. https://doi.org/10.15837/ijccc.2018.6.3356

Alabdan, R. (2020). Phishing attacks survey Types, vectors, and technical approaches. *Future Internet, 12*(10), 168. https://doi.org/10.3390/fi12100168

Al-Eidi, S., Darwish, O., & Chen, Y. (2020). Covert timing channel analysis either as cyberattacks or confidential applications. *Sensors, 20*(8), 2417. https://doi.org/10.3390/s20082417

Alharthi, S., Levy, Y., & Awaji, M. (2019). Empirical Testing of Resistance and Misuse Factors Contributing to Instructors' Use of E-Learning Systems in Saudi Arabia. *AIS Transactions on Replication Research, 5*, 1. https://.doi.org/10.17705/1atrr.00033

Alimbaev, A., Bitenova, B., & Bayandin, M. (2021). Information and communication technologies in the healthcare system of the Republic of Kazakhstan: Economic efficiency and development prospects. *Montenegrin Journal of Economics, 17*(3), 145-156. https://doi.org/10.14254/1800-5845/2021.17-3.12

Amir, E., Levi, S., & Livne, T. (2018). Do firms underreport information on cyberattacks? Evidence from capital markets. *Review of Accounting Studies, 23*(3), 1177-1206. https://doi.org/10.1007/s11142-018-9452-4

Amoroso, E. G. (2013). *Cyberattacks: Protecting national infrastructure*. Waltham, MA: Butterworth-Heinemann/Elsevier

Andress, J. (2011). *The basics of information security: Understanding the fundamentals of InfoSec in theory and practice*. Waltham, MA: Syngress

Arai, K. (2022). *Intelligent Computing: Proceedings of the 2021 Computing Conference, Volume 1*. Springer

Arányi, G., & Dávid, Á. (2021). Introduction of the ARDS—Anti-ransomware defense system Model—Based on the systematic review of worldwide ransomware attacks. *Applied Sciences, 11*(13), 6070. https://doi.org/10.3390/app11136070

Arcuri, M. C., Gai, L., Ielasi, F., & Ventisette, E. (2020). Cyberattacks on hospitality sector: Stock market reaction. *Journal of Hospitality and Tourism Technology, 11*(2), 277-290. https://doi.org/10.1108/JHTT-05-2019-0080

Aruna, B., & Usharani, B. (2020). SQLID framework in order To Perceive SQL injection attacks on a web application. *IOP Conference Series. Materials Science and Engineering, 981*(2). https://doi.org/10.1088/1757-899X/981/2/022013

Ayyagari, R., Lim, J., & Hoxha, O. (2019). Why do we not use password managers? A study on the intention to use password managers. *Contemporary Management Research, 15*(4), 227-234,236-245. https://doi.org/10.7903/cmr.19394

Ballew, Joli. (2011). *Motorola Xoom Companion*. Wiley

Batteau, A. W. (2011). Creating a culture of enterprise cybersecurity. *International Journal of Business Anthropology, 2*(2), 36-47

Bayuk, J. L., & ProQuest (Firm). (2012). *Cybersecurity policy guidebook*. Hoboken, N.J: Wiley

Bonguet, A., & Bellaiche, M. (2017). A survey of denial-of-service and distributed denial of service attacks and defenses in cloud computing. *Future Internet, 9*(3), 43. https://doi.org/10.3390/fi9030043

Boring, R. (2018). *Advances in Human Error, Reliability, Resilience, and Performance: Proceedings of the AHFE 2018 International Conference on Human Error, Reliability, Resilience, and Performance, July 21-25, 2018, Loews Sapphire Falls Resort at Universal Studios, Orlando, Florida, USA*. Springer

Bragg, R. (2003). *CISSP certification: Training guide*. Indianapolis, IN: Que Pub

Buinevich, M., & Vladyko, A. (2019). Forecasting Issues of Wireless Communication Networks' Cyber Resilience for An Intelligent Transportation System: An Overview of Cyber Attacks. *Information, 10*(1), 27. https://doi.org/10.3390/info10010027

Burns, A. J., Posey, C., Courtney, J. F., Roberts, T. L., & Nanayakkara, P. (2017). Organizational information security as a complex adaptive system: Insights from three agent-based models. *Information Systems Frontiers, 19*(3), 509-524. https://doi.org/10.1007/s10796-015-9608-8

Catak, F. O., Ahmed, J., Sahinbas, K., & Zahid, H. K. (2021). Data augmentation-based malware detection using convolutional neural networks. *PeerJ Computer Science*. https://doi.org/10.7717/peerj-cs.346

Charoensukmongkol, P. (2017). Contributions of mindfulness during post-merger integration. *Journal of Managerial Psychology, 32*(1), 104-118. https://dx.doi.org/10.1108/JMP-02-2016-0039

Chen, D., Yan, Q., Wu, C., & Zhao, J. (2021). SQL injection attack detection and prevention techniques using deep learning. *Journal of Physics: Conference Series, 1757*(1) https://doi.org/10.1088/1742-6596/1757/1/012055

Chen, Y., & Wu, H. (2013). Security risks and protection in online learning: A survey. *International Review of Research in Open and Distance Learning, 14*(5).

Chenthara, S., Ahmed, K., & Whittaker, F. (2019). Privacy-preserving data sharing using multi-layer access control model in an electronic health environment. *EAI Endorsed Transactions on Scalable Information Systems, 6*(22). https://doi.org/10.4108/eai.13-7-2018.159356

Chenthara, S., Ahmed, K., Wang, H., Whittaker, F., & Chen, Z. (2020). Health chain: A novel framework on privacy preservation of electronic health records using blockchain technology. *PLoS One, 15*(12). https://doi.org/10.1371/journal.pone.0243043

Chu, W. (2019). Application of Data Encryption Technology in Computer Network Security. *Journal of Physics: Conference Series, 1237*(2). https://doi.org/10.1088/1742-6596/1237/2/022049

Churi, P., Pawar, A., & Moreno-Guerrero, A. (2021). A comprehensive survey on data utility and privacy: Taking Indian healthcare system as a potential case study. *Inventions, 6*(3), 45. https://doi.org/10.3390/inventions6030045

CISA (2021). Cybersecurity Awareness Month. https://www.cisa.gov/cybersecurity-awareness-month

Clarke, J. (2012). *SQL Injection Attacks and Defense.* Elsevier

Cybersecurity Operations (n.d.). NCTOC Top 5 Security Operations Center (SOC) Principles. https://www.nsa.gov/portals/75/documents/resources/cybersecurity-professionals/top-5-soc-principles.pdf

Das, R., & Sandhane, R. (2021). Artificial intelligence in cyber security. *Journal of Physics: Conference Series, 1964*(4). https://doi.org/10.1088/1742-6596/1964/4/042072

Datplan (2019). Cybersecurity (The short guide to get started)

Denning, D. E. (2012). Stuxnet: What has changed? *Future Internet, 4*(3), 672-687. https://doi.org/10.3390/fi4030672

DHS (2011). Preventing and Defending Against Cyber Attacks. https://www.dhs.gov/xlibrary/assets/preventing-and-defending-against-cyberattacks.pdf

Eduardo, B., Walter, F., & Sandra, S. (2020). Characterization of Phishing Attacks and Techniques to Mitigate These Attacks: A Systematic Review of the Literature. *Ciencia y Tecnología, 13*(1), 97-104. https://doi.org/10.18779/cyt.v13i1.357

Electronic Privacy Information Center (2021). Cybersecurity Privacy Practical Implications. https://epic.org/privacy/cybersecurity/

Equifax (2021). The consequences of identity fraud. https://www.equifax.co.uk/resources/articles/the_consequences_of_identity_fraud.html

Equifax, (2021). Your social media profile and identity theft. https://www.equifax.co.uk/resources/identity-protection/your-social-media-profile-and-identity-theft.html

Eze, T. (2021). *ECCWS 2021 20th European Conference on Cyber Warfare and Security*. Academic Conferences Inter Ltd

Fagan, M., Albayram, Y., Khan, M. M., Hasan, & Buck, R. (2017). An investigation into users' considerations towards using password managers. *Human-Centric Computing and Information Sciences, 7*(1), 1-20. https://doi.org/10.1186/s13673-017-0093-6

Fatima, M. A., Moonesar, I. A., & AlQutob, R. (2020). Healthcare Professional and User Perceptions of eHealth Data and Record Privacy in Dubai. *Information, 11*(9), 415. https://doi.org/10.3390/info11090415

Feras, M. A. (2020). Advanced Persistent Threats and its role in Network Security Vulnerabilities. *International Journal of Advanced Research in Computer Science, 11*(1), 11-20. https://doi.org/10.26483/ijarcs.v11i1.6502

Finley, L. L. (2011). *Encyclopedia of school crime and violence*. Santa Barbara, Calif: ABC-CLIO

Forbes Technology Council (2019). Evaluating Your Company's Cybersecurity Strength: 12 Key Indicators. *Forbes*, 18th December 2019. https://www.forbes.com/sites/forbestechcouncil/2019/12/18/evalua ting-your-companys-cybersecurity-strength-12-key-indicators/

Fujdiak, R., Kuchar, K., Holasova, E., & Misurec, J. (2021). Generator of slow denial-of-service cyberattacks. *Sensors, 21*(16), 5473. https://doi.org/10.3390/s21165473

Gao, X., & Zhong, W. (2015). Information security investment for competitive firms with hacker behavior and security requirements. *Annals of Operations Research, 235*(1), 277-300. https://doi.org/10.1007/s10479-015-1925-2

Gao, X., Zhong, W., & Mei, S. (2014). A game-theoretic analysis of information sharing and security investment for complimentary firms. *The Journal of the Operational Research Society, 65*(11), 1682-1691. https://doi.org/10.1057/jors.2013.133

Gavurová, B., Balloni, A. J., Tarhaničová, M., & Kováč, V. (2018). Information and communication technology in the role of the information system of healthcare facility in the Slovak republic. *Economies, 6*(3). https://doi.org/10.3390/economies6030047

Genge, B., Siaterlis, C., & Hohenadel, M. (2012). Impact of network infrastructure parameters on the effectiveness of cyberattacks against industrial control systems. *International Journal of Computers, Communications, and Control, 7*(4), 674-687. https://doi.org/10.15837/ijccc.2012.4.1366

Georgescu, C., & Tudor, M. (2015). Cyberterrorism threats to critical infrastructures NATO's role in cyber defense. *Knowledge Horizons. Economics, 7*(2), 115-118

Gladden, M. E. (2017). Axiology of information security for futuristic neuroprostheses: Upholding human values in the context of technological post-humanization. *Frontiers in Neuroscience.* https://doi.org/10.3389/fnins.2017.00605

Gole, I., Sharma, T., & Misra, S. B. (2017). Role of ICT in the healthcare sector: An empirical study of Pune City. *Journal of Management and Public Policy, 8*(2), 23-32

Good, M. C., & Hyman, M. R. (2020). Protection motivation theory and brick-and-mortar salespeople. *International Journal of Retail & Distribution Management, 48*(8), 865-879. https://doi.org/10.1108/IJRDM-05-2019-0155

Guo, W. (2021). Discuss the security countermeasures and data protection of library computer networks. *Journal of Physics: Conference Series, 1915*(4) https://doi.org/10.1088/1742-6596/1915/4/042049

Haapamäki, E., & Sihvonen, J. (2019). Cybersecurity in accounting research. *Managerial Auditing Journal, 34*(7), 808-834. https://doi.org/10.1108/MAJ-09-2018-2004

Haider, A., Khan, M. A., Rehman, A., Rahman, M. U., & Kim, H. S. (2021). A real-time sequential deep extreme learning machine cybersecurity intrusion detection system. *Computers, Materials, & Continua, 66*(2), 1785-1798. https://doi.org/10.32604/cmc.2020.013910

Halder, S., & Ozdemir, S. (2018). *Hands-on machine learning for cybersecurity: Safeguard your system by making your machines intelligent using the Python ecosystem.* Packet Publishing

He, X. (2021). Research on Computer Network Security Problems and Countermeasures. *Journal of Physics: Conference Series, 1992*(3). https://doi.org/10.1088/1742-6596/1992/3/032069

Hill, J. B., & Marion, N. E. (2016). *Introduction to Cybercrime: Computer Crimes, Laws, and Policing in the 21st Century.* ABC-CLIO

HIPAA (2018). Research Suggests Healthcare Data Breaches Cause 2,100 Deaths a Year. https://www.hipaajournal.com/research-suggests-healthcare-data-breaches-cause-2100-deaths-a-year/

Hrabcak, D., Dobos, L., & Ovsenik, L. (2020). Multilayered Network Model for Mobile Network Infrastructure Disruption. *Sensors, 20*(19), 5491. https://doi.org/10.3390/s20195491

Huang, W. (2021). Design of computer network security defense system based on big data. *Journal of Physics: Conference Series, 1881*(2). https://doi.org/10.1088/1742-6596/1881/2/022049

Hunter, E. S. (2013). Electronic health records in an occupational health setting--part I. A global overview: [1]. *Workplace Health & Safety, 61*(2), 57-60. https://doi.org/10.3928/21650799-20130129-02

Huo, Z. (2019). Computer Network Security Evaluation Based on LM-BP Neural Network. *IOP Conference Series. Earth and Environmental Science, 252*(2). https://doi.org/10.1088/1755-1315/252/2/022012

Hussain, F., Syed, G. A., Shah, G. A., Ivan, M. P., Fayyaz, U. U., Shahzad, F. Zdravevski, E. (2021). A framework for malicious traffic detection in IoT healthcare environment. *Sensors, 21*(9), 3025. https://doi.org/10.3390/s21093025

Hyungjin, L. K., & Han, J. (2019). Do employees in a "good" company comply better with information security policy? A corporate social responsibility perspective. *Information Technology & People, 32*(4), 858-875. https://doi.org/10.1108/ITP-09-2017-0298

IBM (n.d.). Artificial intelligence for a smarter kind of cybersecurity. https://www.ibm.com/security/artificial-intelligence

IBM Cloud Education (2019). What are Security Controls? https://www.ibm.com/cloud/learn/security-controls

Idemudia, E. C. (2019). *Handbook of research on technology integration in the global world.* IGI Global

In Blackburn, A., In Chen, I. L., In Pfeffer, R., & IGI Global (2019). *Emerging trends in cyberethics and education.* IGI Global

In Clark, R. M., & In Hakim, S. (2017). *Cyber-Physical Security: Protecting Critical Infrastructure at the State and Local Level.* Springer

In Gonzalez, J. J., & In Kemp, R. L. (2019). *Cybersecurity: Current writings on threats and protection.* McFarland & Company

In Maleh, Y., In Shojafar, M., In Alazab, M., & In Baddi, Y. (2021). *Machine intelligence and big data analytics for cybersecurity applications*

In Palomares, C. I., In Kalutarage, H. K., & In Huang, Y. (2017). *Data analytics and decision support for cybersecurity: Trends, methodologies, and applications.* Cham: Springer International Publishing

In Shrobe, H. E., In Shrier, D. L., & In Pentland, A. (2017). *New solutions for cybersecurity.* MIT Press

In Thatcher, J., In Eckert, J., & In Shears, A. (2018). *Thinking big data in geography: new regimes, new research.* U of Nebraska Press

In Vasileiou, I., & In Furnell, S. (2019). *Cybersecurity education for awareness and compliance.* IGI Global

Ivanyo, Y. M., Krakovsky, Y. M., & Luzgin, A. N. (2018). Interval forecasting of cyberattacks on industrial control systems. *IOP Conference Series. Materials Science and Engineering, 327*(2) https://doi.org/10.1088/1757-899X/327/2/022044

Jain, A. K., & Gupta, B. B. (2017). Phishing detection: Analysis of visual similarity-based approaches. *Security and Communication Networks, 2017,* 20. http://doi.org/10.1155/2017/5421046

Jang, S., Li, S., & Sung, Y. (2020). Fast Text-based local feature visualization algorithm for merged image-based malware classification framework for Cybersecurity and cyber defense. *Mathematics, 8*(3), 460. https://doi.org/10.3390/math8030460

Jasiul, B., Szpyrka, M., & Sliwa, J. (2014). Detection and modeling of cyberattacks with Petri nets. *Entropy, 16*(12), 6602-6623. https://doi.org/10.3390/e16126602

Jensen, E. T. (2010). Cyberwarfare and precautions against the effects of attacks. *Texas Law Review, 88*(7), 1533-1569

Jiang, J. (2021). Computer Network Security Threats and Treatment Measures Based on Host Security Protection. *Journal of Physics: Conference Series, 1992*(3). https://doi.org/10.1088/1742-6596/1992/3/032049

Kadivar, M. (2014). Cyberattack attributes. *Technology Innovation Management Review, 4*(11), 22-27

Kavallieratos, C. & Katsikas, S. (2020). Managing Cybersecurity risks of the cyber-enabled ship. (2020). *Journal of Marine Science and Engineering, 8*(10), 768. https://doi.org/10.3390/jmse8100768

Kim, K., Alfouzan, F. A., & Kim, H. (2021). Cyberattack scoring model based on the offensive cybersecurity framework. *Applied Sciences, 11*(16), 7738. https://doi.org/10.3390/app11167738

Klein, J. J. (2015). Deterring and dissuading cyberterrorism. *Journal of Strategic Security, 8*(4), 23-38. https://doi.org/10.5038/1944-0472.8.4.1460

Koczkodaj, W. W., Mazurek, M., Strzałka, D., Wolny-Dominiak, A., & Woodbury-Smith, M. (2019). Electronic Health Record Breaches as Social Indicators. *Social Indicators Research, 141*(2), 861-871. https://doi.org/10.1007/s11205-018-1837-z

Krstic, B., PhD., & Krstic, M., PhD. (2015). Rational choice theory and random behavior. *Ekonomika, 61*(1), 1-13

Kshetri, N. (2013). Cybercrime and cyber-security issues associated with China: Some economic and institutional considerations. *Electronic Commerce Research, 13*(1), 41-69. https://doi.org/10.1007/s10660-013-9105-4

Kwiatkowska, E. M. (2016). IT solutions for a healthcare system in Poland: In search of benchmarks in various economic perspectives. *Economics & Sociology, 9*(3), 210-223. https://doi.org/10.14254/2071789X.2016/9-3/18

Lee, N. (2013). *Counterterrorism and cybersecurity: total information awareness.* New York, NY: Springer

Leukfeldt, E. R., Lavorgna, A., & Kleemans, E. R. (2017). Organized cybercrime or cybercrime that is organized? An assessment of the conceptualization of financial cybercrime as organized crime. *European Journal on Criminal Policy and Research, 23*(3), 287-300. https://doi.org/10.1007/s10610-016-9332-z

Levy, Y., Ramim, M. M., & Hackney, R. A. (2013). Assessing ethical severity of e-learning systems security attacks. *The Journal of Computer Information Systems, 53*(3), 75-84

Li, Y., & Zhang, B. (2019). Detection of SQL injection attacks based on improved TFIDF algorithm. *Journal of Physics: Conference Series, 1395*(1). https://doi.org/10.1088/1742-6596/1395/1/012013

Li, Y., Xiong, K., & Li, X. (2019). Applying machine learning techniques to understand user behaviors when phishing attacks occur. *EAI Endorsed Transactions on Security and Safety, 6*(21) https://doi.org/10.4108/eai.13-7-2018.162809

Limba, T., Plėta, T., Agafonov, K., & Damkus, M. (2017). Cybersecurity management model for critical infrastructure. *Entrepreneurship and Sustainability Issues, 4*(4), 559-573. https://doi.org/10.9770/jesi.2017.4.4(12)

Luca, G. (2017). Manifestations of contemporary terrorism: Cyberterrorism. *Research and Science Today,* (1), 20-25

Luo, G. (2020). Research on computer network security problems and protective measures under the background of big data. *Journal of Physics: Conference Series, 1607*(1) https://doi.org/10.1088/1742-6596/1607/1/012092

Macdonald, S., Jarvis, L. & Lavis, S. (2019). Cyberterrorism Today? Findings From a Follow-on Survey of Researchers. *Studies in Conflict & Terrorism.* https://doi.org/10.1080/1057610X.2019.1696444

Mahfouz, A., Abuhussein, A., Venugopal, D., & Shiva, S. (2020). Ensemble classifiers for network intrusion detection using a novel network attack dataset. *Future Internet, 12*(11), 180. https://doi.org/10.3390/fi12110180

Maitra, A. K. (2015). Offensive cyber-weapons: Technical, legal, and strategic aspects. *Environment Systems & Decisions, 35*(1), 169-182. https://doi.org/10.1007/s10669-014-9520-7

Management Association & Information Resources (2021). *Research Anthology on Business Aspects of Cybersecurity.* IGI Global

Manoj, K. S. (2020). *Cyber Security.* Notion Press

Marsili, M. (2018). The War on Cyberterrorism. *Democracy and Security.* https://doi.org/10.1080/17419166.2018.1496826

Mehan, J. E. (2014). *Cyberwar, cyberterrorism, cybercrime, and cyberactivism: An in-depth guide to the role of security standards in the cybersecurity environment, 2nd edition.* Ely, Cambridgeshire, U.K: IT Governance Pub

Mentsiev, A. U., Magomadov, V. S., Ashakhanova, M. Z., & Alams, M. T. (2019). How the development of blockchain affected cybersecurity. *Journal of Physics: Conference Series, 1399*(3). https://doi.org/10.1088/1742-6596/1399/3/033048

Mentsiev, A. U., Magomadov, V. S., Ashakhanova, M. Z., & Alams, M. T. (2019). How the development of blockchain affected cybersecurity. *Journal of Physics: Conference Series, 1399*(3). https://doi.org/10.1088/1742-6596/1399/3/033048

Miller, R. L. R., & Meinzinger, M. (2016). *Paralegal Today: The legal team at work.* Cengage Learning

Miron, W., & Muita, K. (2014). Cybersecurity capability maturity models for providers of critical infrastructure. *Technology Innovation Management Review, 4*(10), 33-39

Misra, S., & Adewumi, A. (2019). *Handbook of Research on the Role of Human Factors in IT Project Management.* Hershey: IGI Global

Mohamed, A. (2020). The Role of Health Concerns in Phishing Susceptibility: Survey Design Study. *Journal of Medical Internet Research, 22*(5). https://doi.org/10.2196/18394

Mohammadi, F. (2021). Emerging Challenges in Smart Grid Cybersecurity Enhancement: A Review. *Energies, 14(5).* https://doi.org/10.3390/en14051380

Morel, B. (2021). *Cyber Insecurity*. Page Publishing Inc.

National Cybersecurity Center. Device Security Guidance. https://www.ncsc.gov.uk/collection/device-security-guidance/policies-and-settings/antivirus-and-other-security-software

National Research Council (U.S.)., National Research Council (U.S.)., National Research Council (U.S.)., & National Research Council (U.S.). (2010). *Proceedings of a workshop on deterring cyberattacks: Informing strategies and developing options for U.S. policy*. Washington, D.C: National Academies Press

North Country Savings Bank (2021). How Oversharing on social media Can Lead to Identity Theft. https://www.northcountrysavings.bank/neighbor-news/how-oversharing-social-media-can-lead-identity-theft

OLĂNESCU, S. S., & OLĂNESCU, A. V. (2019). Cyberterrorism: The latest crime against international public order. *Lex Et Scientia, Xxvi* (1)

Ortner, D. (2015). Cybercrime and punishment: The Russian mafia and Russian responsibility to exercise due diligence to prevent transboundary cybercrime. *Brigham Young University Law Review, 2015*(1), 177-217

Park, J., Loia, V., Yi, G. & Sung, Y. (2017). *Advances in Computer Science and Ubiquitous Computing: CSA-CUTE 17*. Springer

Pascale, F., Adinolfi, E. A., Coppola, S., & Santonicola, E. (2021). Cybersecurity in automotive: An intrusion detection system in connected vehicles. *Electronics, 10*(15), 1765. https://doi.org/10.3390/electronics10151765

Patterson, D. (2021). Schools have become the leading targets of ransomware attacks. *CBS News*, 11th March 2021. https://www.cbsnews.com/news/schools-popular-ransomware-targets/. Accessed on 20/9/2021

Peltier, T. (2004). *Information Security Policies and Procedures: A Practitioner's Reference, Second*. CRC Press

Peterson, L. L., & Davie, B. S. (2012). *Computer networks: A systems approach*. Burlington, MA: Morgan Kaufmann

Pooser, D. M., Browne, M. J., & Arkhangelska, O. (2018). Growth in the perception of cyber risk: Evidence from U.S. P&C insurers. *Geneva Papers on Risk & Insurance, 43*(2), 208-223. https://doi.org/10.1057/s41288-017-0077-9

Potkin, F. (2020). FACTBOX-Major hacks of social media platforms. *Reuters*, 16th July 2020. https://www.reuters.com/article/twitter-cyber-idUSL2N2EN073

Querolo, N. & Singh, S. (2021). Schools Brace for More Cyberattacks After Record in 2020. *BBC News*, 9th August 2021. https://www.bloomberg.com/news/features/2021-08-09/schools-brace-for-more-cyberattacks-after-record-2020. Accessed on 20/9/2021

Radvanovsky, R. & McDougall, A. (2013). *Critical Infrastructure: Homeland Security and Emergency Preparedness, Third Edition*. CRC Press

Rao, F. A., Dominic, P. D. D., Syed Emad, A. A., Rehman, M., & Sohail, A. (2021). Information security behavior and information security policy compliance: A systematic literature review for identifying the transformation process from non-compliance to compliance. *Applied Sciences, 11*(8), 3383. https://doi.org/10.3390/app11083383

Rastenis, J., Ramanauskaitė, S., Janulevičius, J., Čenys, A., Slotkienė, A., & Pakrijauskas, K. (2020). E-mail-based phishing attack taxonomy. *Applied Sciences, 10*(7), 2363. https://doi.org/10.3390/app10072363

Ray, A., & Kaushik, A. (2017). State transgression on electronic expression: Is it for real? *Information and Computer Security, 25*(4), 382-401. https://doi.org/10.1108/ICS-03-2016-0024

Reddy, P. V., Sridhar, A., Mishra, V. K., & Aditya, M. (2021). Cascading effects of cyberattacks on interconnected critical infrastructure. *Cybersecurity, 4*(1). https://doi.org/10.1186/s42400-021-00071-z

Romancheva, N. I. (2021). Duality of artificial intelligence technologies in assessing Cybersecurity risk. *IOP Conference Series. Materials Science and Engineering, 1069*(1) https://doi.org/10.1088/1757-899X/1069/1/012004

Rose, B., Bowsher, G., & Sullivan, R. (2020). Cybersecurity and the unexplored threat to global health: A call for global norms. *Global Security: Health, Science and Policy, 5*(1), 134-141. https://doi.org/10.1080/23779497.2020.1865182

Sales, N. A. (2013). Regulating cyber-security. *Northwestern University Law Review, 107*(4), 1503-1568.

Sarkar, K. (2018). *SQL Injection Best Method for Beginners*. Smash words Edition

Sarker, I. H. (2019). Context-aware rule learning from smartphone data: Survey, challenges and future directions. *Journal of Big Data, 6*(1), 1-25. https://doi.org/10.1186/s40537-019-0258-4

Sarker, I. H., Hamed, A., Fawaz, A., Khan, A. I., Abushark, Y. B., & Siddiqui, M. K. (2020). Context pre-modeling: An empirical analysis for classification-based user-centric context-aware predictive modeling. *Journal of Big Data, 7*(1). https://doi.org/10.1186/s40537-020-00328-3

Sarker, I. H., Kayes, A. S. M., Shahriar, B., Hamed, A., Watters, P., & Ng, A. (2020). Cybersecurity data science: An overview from machine learning perspective. *Journal of Big Data, 7*(1). https://doi.org/10.1186/s40537-020-00318-5

Sechel, S. (2019). A comparative assessment of obfuscated ransomware detection methods. *Informatica Economica, 23*(2), 45-62

Sidi, B. E., Mrabet, H., Gharbi, H., Jemai, A., & Trentesaux, D. (2020). A survey on the usage of blockchain technology for cyber-threats in the context of industry 4.0. *Sustainability, 12*(21), 9179. http://doi.org/10.3390/su12219179

Sidi, B. E., Mrabet, H., Gharbi, H., Jemai, A., & Trentesaux, D. (2020). A survey on the usage of blockchain technology for cyber-threats in the context of industry 4.0. *Sustainability, 12*(21), 9179. https://doi.org/10.3390/su12219179

Sikolia, D., Twitchell, D., & Sagers, G. (2018). Protection motivation and deterrence: Evidence from a Fortune 100 company. *AIS Transactions on Replication Research, 4*, 7. https://doi.org/10.17705/1atrr.00027

Skinner, C. P. (2019). Bank disclosures of cyber exposure. *Iowa Law Review, 105*(1), 239-281

Sommestad, T., Hallberg, J., Lundholm, K., & Bengtsson, J. (2014). Variables influencing information security policy compliance: A systematic review of quantitative studies. *Information Management & Computer Security, 22*(1), 42-75. https://doi.org/10.1108/IMCS-08-2012-0045

Spellman, F. R., & Stoudt, M. L. (2011). *Nuclear infrastructure protection and homeland security*. Lanham, MD: Government Institutes

Steingartner, W., Galinec, D., & Kozina, A. (2021). Threat defense: Cyber deception approach and education for resilience in hybrid threats model. *Symmetry, 13*(4), 597. https://doi.org/10.3390/sym13040597

Stevenson, S. (2004). Recognizing and preparing loss estimates from cyberattacks. *Information Systems Security, 12*(6), 46-57

Stewart, J. (2020). *Network Security, Firewalls, and VPNs*. Place of publication not identified: Jones & Bartlett Learning

Sun, X. D., Ren, Z., Yang, P. W., Li, J., Chen, H. Y., & Liu, T. Q. (2019). Artificial intelligence design research on the Cybersecurity penetration testing of power grid enterprises. *IOP Conference Series. Earth and Environmental Science, 354*(1). https://doi.org/10.1088/1755-1315/354/1/012104

Tariq, N. (2018). Impact of cyberattacks on financial institutions. *Journal of Internet Banking and Commerce, 23*(2), 1-11

Tellbach, D., & Yan-Fu, L. (2018). Cyberattacks on smart meters in household nano grid: Modeling, simulation, and analysis. *Energies, 11*(2), 316. https://doi.org/10.3390/en11020316

Tidy, J. (2021). How your personal data is being scraped from social media. *BBC News*, 16th July 2021. https://www.bbc.com/news/business-57841239

Tidy, J. (2021). School cyberattack affects 40,000 pupils' email. https://www.bbc.com/news/technology-56569873. Accessed on 20/9/2021

Tsohou, A., & Holtkamp, P. (2018). Are users competent to comply with information security policies? An analysis of professional competence models. *Information Technology & People, 31*(5), 1047-1068. https://doi.org/10.1108/ITP-02-2017-0052

Vartolomei, C., & Avasilcăi, S. (2020). Digitalization concept: Cyber-risks and damages for companies in adhered industries. *IOP Conference Series. Materials Science and Engineering, 898*(1). https://doi.org/10.1088/1757-899X/898/1/012044

Waleed, A. A. (2019). An effective multifactor authentication mechanism based on combiners of hash function over the internet of things. *Sensors, 19*(17), 3663. http://doi.org/10.3390/s19173663

Walmor Cristino, L. J., Claudio Coreixas, d. M., Carlos E P de, A., Santos Machado, R. C., & Oliveira de Sá, A. (2021). A triggering mechanism for cyberattacks in naval sensors and systems. *Sensors, 21*(9), 3195. https://doi.org/10.3390/s21093195

Wang, C., Ren, T., Li, Q., Wang, X., Guo, G., & Dong, J. (2020). Network computer security hidden dangers and vulnerability mining technology. *IOP Conference Series. Materials Science and Engineering, 750*(1). https://doi.org/10.1088/1757-899X/750/1/012155

Wang, D., & Liu, H. (2021). Application of computer network security information encryption technology. *Journal of Physics: Conference Series, 1992*(2) https://doi.org/10.1088/1742-6596/1992/2/022094

Wang, J., Zhang, H., Wu, Z., & Xu, G. (2020). Research on computer network teaching reform based on simulation software. *Journal of Physics: Conference Series, 1654*(1) https://doi.org/10.1088/1742-6596/1654/1/012127

Wang, Z., Yao, Y., Tong, X., Luo, Q., & Chen, X. (2019). Dynamically reconfigurable encryption and decryption system design for the internet of things information security. *Sensors, 19*(1). http://doi.org/10.3390/s19010143

Weidong, F., Chen, W., Wuxiong, Z., Pei, J., Weiwei, G., & Wang, G. (2020). Digital signature scheme for information non-repudiation in the blockchain: A state of the art review. *EURASIP Journal on Wireless Communications and Networking, 2020*(1). https://doi.org/10.1186/s13638-020-01665-w

Weimann, G. (2004). Cyberterrorism How Real Is the Threat? *United States Institute of Peace*

Weisbaum, H. (2019). How to create strong passwords you can remember. https://www.nbcnews.com/better/tech/how-create-strong-passwords-you-can-remember-ncna958416

White, G. (2021). General population demographics of responses to a nationwide catastrophic cyberattack: Exploratory research. *Journal of International Technology and Information Management, 30*(1), 1-29,1A-1B

Wilcox, H., & Bhattacharya, M. (2020). A human dimension of hacking: Social engineering through social media. *IOP Conference Series. Materials Science and Engineering, 790*(1) https://doi.org/10.1088/1757-899X/790/1/012040

Wilcox, H., & Bhattacharya, M. (2020). A human dimension of hacking: Social engineering through social media. *IOP Conference Series. Materials Science and Engineering, 790*(1) https://doi.org/10.1088/1757-899X/790/1/012040

Wu, H., Ash, I., Anwar, M., Li, L., Yuan, X., Xu, L., & Tian, X. (2020). Improving employees' intellectual capacity for cybersecurity through evidence-based malware training. *Journal of Intellectual Capital, 21*(2), 203-213. https://doi.org/10.1108/JIC-05-2019-0112

Zhang, X., Liu, S., Wang, L., Zhang, Y., & Wang, J. (2020). Mobile health service adoption in China: Integration of theory of planned behavior, protection motivation theory and personal health differences. *Online Information Review, 44*(1), 1-23. https://doi.org/10.1108/OIR-11-2016-0339

Zhao, J., & Liu, C. (2020). Design and implementation of SQL injection vulnerability scanning tool. *Journal of Physics: Conference Series, 1575*(1). https://doi.org/10.1088/1742-6596/1575/1/012094

Zhiwen, P., Jesus, P., Salim, H., Yiqiang, C. & Bozhi, L. (2019). Context-Aware Anomaly Behavior Analysis for Smart Home Systems. *International Journal of Information and Communication Technology, 13(5)*

Dr. Tunde Alaofin

ABOUT THE AUTHOR

D r. Tunde Alaofin is an Associate Professor in the School of Cybersecurity & Information Technology at the University of Maryland Global Campus. In addition to his academic position, he is the President & CEO of Delexis Healthcare Solutions incorporated and a former franchisee & Chief Technology Officer of Geeks On Call Corporation in Washington, DC Metro.

Dr. Alaofin is a Systems & Software Engineer with over 25 years of experience in Artificial Intelligence Systems, Cloud Computing, Healthcare Management Capacity Building, and Assistive Technology implementation for Corporate America and United States Governmental Agencies including the Department of Health & Human Services, the United States Department of Agriculture, and the Social Security Administration.

Dr. Alaofin served as an Assistant Director of Information Systems at the University of South Carolina from 1994 to 1997, and as Senior Director of Technology at LightTrade Corporation in Washington, DC from 1999 to 2002. Dr. Alaofin earned a doctorate in Information Technology from Walden University, a master's degree in Computer Science from Georgia Southwestern State University, and a bachelor's degree in Business and Information Systems Management from Allen University and the University of South Carolina.

Artificial Intelligence Systems, Machine Learning, and Software Engineering are among his research interests. Dr. Alaofin is the author of two books and several publications in scholarly journals. He is a member of the Association for the Advancement of Artificial Intelligence and the Association for the Advancement of Computational Intelligence (AAAI). Dr. Alaofin is a mentor as well as an entrepreneur.

Lightning Source UK Ltd.
Milton Keynes UK
UKHW022035150223
417099UK00025B/317/J